MOLE NOTES

MICHAEL BENEDIKT

MOLE NOTES

WESLEYAN UNIVERSITY PRESS

Middletown, Connecticut

Paperback: ISBN: 0-8195-6018-9
Hardbound: ISBN: 0-8195-4038-2
Library of Congress Catalog Card Number: 78-161695
Manufactured in the United States of America
First edition

CONTENTS

VI

II. THE MAKING OF LOVE

III. THE POWER PEOPLE

VIII

ILLUSTRATIONS

Mole renderings on end papers and elsewhere are reproduced by
courtesy of the New York Public Library.

Western Mole · *Scapanus townsendii* · Talpidae

FROM northern Mexico to southwestern British Columbia, and east to central Oregon and Washington and western Nevada, is the range of a group of moles sometimes spoken of collectively as the Western moles. It is sometimes difficult for anyone except a specialist to tell one from another. The Townsend mole, however, occupies the range north of California; the California mole extends its range northward only into extreme southern Oregon; and the Pacific mole matches the range of the Townsend mole and covers the northern haunts of the California mole. Of these three, the Townsend mole is the largest and most beautiful. It is nearly 9 inches long, including 2-inch tail, is almost wholly black, and weighs to 6 ounces. The Pacific mole occasionally reaches a length of 6¾ inches, including ½-inch tail.

Male Townsend moles are longer than the females by nearly an inch. The fur is paler on the underside, with a brown tinge, and the animals are lighter in winter.

Western moles are rather solitary except in the breeding season, when a tunnel may be used by a number of them. The nest is in a cavern deep underground and is lined with dry grass and leaves. Mating is in late winter and the 2–4 young are born about a month later. Adult size and independence are reached in early summer or June. There is but 1 litter a year.

The food of Western moles is largely the larvae of insects, earthworms, and other soft-bodied animals to be found in the habitat. One record indicates that 1 Western mole in just over 2 months made more than 300 earth mounds in a field of ¼ acre. This definitely suggests the role moles play in aerating the soil. Probably most of the damage to crops charged against moles is really the work of mice, which run through the burrows to feed on exposed root crops. Of course a molehill on a golf putting green has its disadvantages, but it is possible that a golf putting green does not represent the best possible use of good agricultural soil. Control of moles is usually through trapping and the use of poison baits and poison gases.

Hairy-tailed Mole or Brewer's Mole
Parascalops breweri · Talpidae

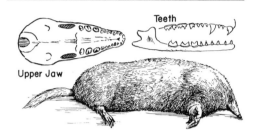

AN area beginning with the Appalachian Highlands in northern Georgia and extending northeast into Ontario and New Brunswick represents the range of this husky mole. It is found at elevations of to 3,000 feet, and is often more abundant than is apparent.

Hairy-tailed moles are to 7 inches long, including a 1⅕ inch tail. Weight, to 3 ounces. The sexes are about equal in size and are similarly colored. The tail is smallest at the base, and hairy, and the snout is coarse and shorter than in the common mole (next page). There is but 1 species in the genus.

The fur is blackish, rather than gray as with common moles. Weight, to 3 ounces. Teeth are: I 3/3; C 1/1; P 4/4; M 3/3. The front feet are about as wide as they are long.

The food, of course, is largely insects and earthworms; a hairy mole may eat its weight in earthworms daily. The major food at some seasons may be the larvae of such beetles as the May beetle, which destroy so much plant material useful to man. Moles may leave their burrows and wander about on top of the ground in search of food. Under such circumstances they are ready prey for cats and other animals. They may also eat ants and other small animals, some of which are enemies of man.

Mating takes place in February or March. From 4–6 weeks later 4–5 young are born. These are blind, helpless, and naked except for a few whiskers, and each weighs about ⅓ ounce. At 4 weeks the young are weaned and become independent. Sexual maturity is reached at the first succeeding breeding season, and old age is reached within 4 years if the animals survive that long.

An individual probably will not know a home range in excess of 100 feet across, and 2 animals to the acre is considered a good population.

Common Mole · *Scalops aquaticus* · Talpidae

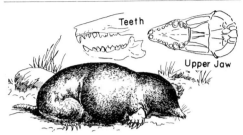

THE term "common" is always dangerous because what may be common in one place may be rare in another. This mole is common from southern Texas north almost to Montana and east to the Atlantic, except for the northern Dakota area, northern Minnesota, Wisconsin, New York, and New England. It varies in color over the range, being gray in the North and brown to copper in the Southwest. The young are usually gray.

Males may measure 9 inches, including a 1⅛ inch tail; females, 8 inches with a 1-inch tail. Weight, to 2 ounces. Tail is naked, or apparently so. There are no external ears, and the eyes are skin covered. The forefeet are broader than they are long, and the snout naked, with upward-pointing nostrils. Teeth are: I 3/2; C 1/0; P 3/3; M 3/3. The fur is finer and softer than that of the hairy-tailed mole.

These moles do not make molehills of excavated earth so commonly as do some of their relatives. They are active in tunnels at all seasons and times of the day, but in winter in the North the tunnels used are often deeper than those of the summer. One dug over 100 feet of tunnels in one day.

Common moles may dig 15 feet in an hour, eat at least half their weight in food daily. Normal population, about 2 or 3 to an acre in suitable territory. They rarely come to the surface, but when they do, they fall easy prey to many enemies. Because of their strong odor they are not commonly eaten by animals that kill them.

In the early spring breeding season 2 or more moles may be found in the same tunnel. Young are born probably 6 weeks after the mating takes place. The 2–6 young in the 1 annual litter are naked and helpless at birth. In 10 days they have a hair covering which is replaced a few weeks later with another coat. The young become independent when about 1 month old and breed at about 10 months of age. The nest is in a grass-lined, 5- to 8-inch den. Food is 50% insects, 30% earthworms, and some plants. Temperature, 94°–100° F.

Star-nosed Mole · *Condylura cristata* · Talpidae

STAR-NOSED moles are found in damp ground from southern Labrador to southeastern Manitoba and south to Georgia and Illinois. There is 1 species in the genus.

If you have ever explored the mud for something lost in it and have used all 5 fingers of your hand to help you, you have a slight idea of what star-nosed moles do much of the time. If you had all your fingers and toes on one hand to work with, you still would not be equipped as is the mole. The snout of a star-nosed mole has 22 fingerlike structures which it uses to explore the mud in which it finds most of its food of earthworms and insect larvae.

Male star-nosed moles are to 8¼ inches long, including a 3⅛ inch tail that is enlarged in the middle with stored fat, and constricted at the base. The tail swelling is greatest in winter. Weight, to 3 ounces. The eyes function, unlike those of most moles. The hind feet measure just over 1 inch, and there are 44 teeth. Teeth are: I 3/3; C 1/1; P 4/4; M 3/3. Both males and females are blackish-brown to black above and paler brown beneath. The legs are weak; the front feet, while wide, are not so large as those of common moles.

Star-nosed moles may live in the same area, and even in the same tunnels, that harbor other species of moles. They are active day or night throughout the year, sometimes in groups. Their hearing is excellent. Their sense of contact is superior, but of smell poor. Their food is about 50% earthworms and 33% insects, the rest of it being miscellaneous.

Mating may take place in the fall and wintering may be in pairs. Females breed when 10 months old. Height of breeding, however, is in January, and 3–6 young are born from mid-April to mid-June. At birth the young are pink, hairless, and helpless. First fur appears in 10 days and a full coat by 3 weeks, when the nest and parent are abandoned. These moles swim well, spend much time above ground, and can give a frightened squeak. About 2 star-nosed moles to an acre is normal, although there may be many more.

THE BIRTH OF MOLE

Mole this morning is a trembling antenna, straining to hear what will be, but beginning modestly with what he will be. You can tell what an effort this existence is by watching the quivering of his whiskers. With the first sound, he starts up from the underground; and as he is born, he forms. Besides his first few trembling antennae, consisting so far of fourteen whiskers out of a possible fifty, one can also see a pair of eyes heavily curtained against incursions of the sun; a pink nose, shaped like a star; one inner ear; a half a thick back foot, and — back at the other end again — two front paws, lighter in color than the rest of the body parts so far, but curiously flexible and delicate, as if a human hand had been inexplicably shaped for some subterranean labor. Perhaps when properly born he might accept a secretarial position with a publishing firm? — typing, taking occasional dictation, and trying hard not to track in mud all over the carpet in the outer office? Still, it's hard to imagine him sitting on the boss's lap! While I was saying all that, at the rear of his tunnel a tail was just formed. How come Mole is growing so fast? It's because two things produce alteration in an actual mole: it's true that a mole grows whenever he senses something that will be; but it's also true that he grows whenever he misses a transmission regarding what is, or what has been. But how can he go on in this condition — how can he proceed without seeing? And how is it that I can see him, since he is obviously invisible from where I live, here on the earth? Mole can go on because his eyesight is famous for excluding the visual as a necessary component of vision; and as for me, I admit I am feeling my way. All this reminds me of the famous passage of Bishop Berkeley: this is the one in which the Bishop says that if a tree falls in the forest with nobody around to hear, it may be that it makes no sound. But Mole's coalescing presence extends the Bishop's proposition to suggest that not only was there no sound if nobody was around, but possibly the tree never fell, because there may have been no tree and no forest in the first place, much less a reliable ear as yet. But if Mole rises from the underground like some kind of new little angel, how long can I go on this way? I'm just about to answer my own query, perhaps with one of the exquisitely polished sonnets or impeccable heroic couplets for which I am well-known, when suddenly the subterranean scraping and scratching discontinues. Has Mole vanished, just as mysteriously as he appeared? Of course not: the sound starts up again, and he must be working harder because it's getting louder and closer; and then Mole flies right up through the earth wall in a burst of dirt and fur! My first reaction: O Mole, go back again; you've come through too soon—; it's awful! You're not complete yet!

It's true too: besides the tail and the fifty little whiskers, all I can see now are two eyes and four paws, the two missing inner, as well as outer, ears; and he would be perfect except that he's still missing a shoulderbone, a nostril, six ribs, and part of a pelvic region. The missing fragments are indicated by dotted lines, as in a diagram. I'm just about to insist that Mole vanish altogether again when suddenly I feel a damp, bristling muzzle slip itself ingratiatingly into my palm. A complete, panting head lies down in my hand! Quick — to the dictionary for the rest of his definition! But already the earth is sifting down behind him, packing in the space for good behind his ever-changing form.

DEFINITIONS FROM BUFFON
(order Insectivora)

Although it is not blind, the mole has eyes that are so tiny, so heavily lidded, that it is unable to make any particular use of the sense of sight: to compensate, nature has given it an extremely delicate sense of touch. Its fur is soft as silk; its hearing is acute, its features include dainty five-fingered hands quite unlike the arm extremities of other animals and nearly identical to the hands of Man; it has a disproportionate degree of strength considering the volume of its body, an exceedingly durable skin, a regularly-maintained rotundity; gentle habits of solitude and repose; it commands the art of establishing a secure space for itself, of creating for itself in an instant a sanctuary and a habitation; facility in enlarging its domain and of finding therein, without exploration of the exterior surface, an abundant sustenance. And this is its entire nature, its credo, comfort, and talent — doubtless preferable to qualities which may be more sparklingly apparent, but also less compatible with true happiness than the darkest and most obscure depths. It seals off the entrances to its retreat, never leaving except when absolutely forced to by an excess of summer rain, when water enters it; or when the gardener's clumsy foot breaks through its domed ceiling. It carves out a rounded vault in the open field; but when in gardens, most often a long tunnel, because it finds it easier to dig into a loose, more cultivated earth than a hard expanse of root-filled area. It thrives neither in thick mud nor in the rockier, more tightly-packed textures of earth: it requires a softer soil, well stocked with succulent roots and most of all populated with the common insects and worms, which it regards as its principal nourishment.

— from Oeuvres de Buffon: L' Histoire Naturelle:
Animaux Domestiques, Carnassiers et Rongeurs (ca. 1770)

SOCIAL CONCERNS

Waking, Mole's greatest social concern at present is this large rock. The earth must have rolled around until the mouth of his burrow was directly under it; then it stopped.

OF THE DIFFICULTY OF FINDING A FRIEND

Mole tries to find a friend. What is the best way to go about such a thing? A mole figures out an answer for himself. Circling around the underground part of the large rock, he digs a long, long tunnel, and comes up right in the middle of a large garden party in Scarsdale. The conversation is certainly interesting: one man is delivering an impromptu monologue regarding his collection of antique pornographic beer steins, all picturing episodes from the Satyricon, and none weighing less than fifty pounds or liftable without the help of three hands or two friends. A lady dressed in dark furs is whispering to another lady about her new lover, a dynamite manufacturer, and also about a new set of exploding golf clubs she has just secretly given her husband's habitual caddy. Yet another lady is rubbing her legs together and referring, in a way she thinks is wittily detached, to a new T.V. star everyone calls "The Poison Dirigible." It is around this time that it occurs to Mole that he might not have too much in common with these interesting inhabitants of Scarsdale. He is about to turn around in his tunnel and go back home, using the route beneath the toolshed, when suddenly he thinks of a sure-fire way to start a conversation. A hopeful, friendly smile on his face, he pops up in the middle of a circle of three ladies with plates on their laps. Very politely, he asks: "Would anybody here like to come down sometime and see my worm collection?" Evidently not; suddenly he feels an empty hors d'oeuvres tray whizz past his whiskers; and so not only does he have to withdraw abruptly from his debut in social conversation, but all that night he has to listen to the sound of rakes, hoes, and shovels pounding down on the roof of his home; the sound of spades digging up almost the entire lawn; and the sound of cars backing up with hoses attached to their tailpipes, filling every hole in the ground with carbon monoxide exhaust, while he sits quietly in the tunnel beneath the toolshed, quaking.

THE WORM COLLECTION

"Psst, psst; hey mister, want to have a look at my worm collection?" No, that's not right; Mole decides that at the next garden party he attends his invitation should be somewhat more genteel. Or more delicately phrased. Perhaps it ought to be in verse? Maybe rhymed — possibly in sonnet form? Also, to make the visit of all his prospective guests more enjoyable, he decides to neaten up his worm collection. Working from an old map he found weeks ago in a garage, he arranges them into a pattern which is an exact replica of the streets of downtown Pittsburgh, Pa., in 1927. Then he surrounds the entrance to the main wormroom with exactly the same patterns an old lady might crochet around the edge of a doily — a design he originally found in an old issue of *Family Circle* stuck in a floorboard crack in a long-deserted gazebo. Then Mole leans back and waits for his first guests. But after several weeks pass, and the first guests fail to arrive, a painful thought crosses Mole's mind: perhaps it is not the style of his invitation which is at fault, but rather his beloved worm collection itself whose beauty nobody appreciates? Could such a thing be possible? At the thought, Mole breaks down and weeps. After only a few more weeks he begins to lose interest in friends; and after a couple of months, the only persons who come to see his map of the outlines of Pittsburgh (now impossibly blurry anyway, due to the movement of the worms) are two lost field mice and a gopher; and these he drives off with angry cries.

IN THE DUNGEONS OF THE SUN

Mole's commitment to holes grows philosophical; he says he resides in a tunnel to escape what he calls "the dungeons of the sun." Sometimes he dramatizes the intellectual content of his acts by standing around under the ground wearing boots and a long cape, with a big "M.E." stitched to his tank-top T-shirt. When magazine interviewers ask on behalf of their vast interested reading public what "M.E." stands for, he snaps back at them: "It stands for Mole," he says, "Mole, the Earth-submarine."

ECOLOGY AND MOLES

One day, as three cars with hoses on their tailpipes are backing up toward several holes he has made at the edge of a particularly scenic parking lot, Mole finally finds a reference to himself in a book: "Although one or two Moles are useful to the ecological survival of nearly every plot of earth on earth, Moles nevertheless fall victim by the millions every year to those who resent the fact that they are apt to create unsightly tunnels in suburban lawns and also leave excavations in expensive golf greens." Then Mole weeps another tunnelful of tears, not for himself this time, but this time for his assassinated brothers among Moles and men, and for the deserted earth, while a chorus of cars angrily gun their engines overhead.

MOLAR MANIFESTO
Or, OF ALL THE ANIMAL KINGDOM
NOT EXCLUDING MOLES

(1) In order for this terrible ecological and other personal and environmental violation to end, it is necessary first of all for men to end assumptions about their domination over living kingdoms other than their own. After all, as things now stand, the vegetable kingdom has more of a future than man does — or, rather, than most men do. (2) Just as man can no longer go on making general assumptions about the superiority of his race to animals, a man can no longer assume, specifically, that there aren't many Animals which are actually superior to some men. (3) To sum up so far: man's earth-abuse is only the final, ecological outcome of a difficulty that is at base psychological and philosophical. It is therefore a mistake to assume that it is at the beginning of this analysis, rather than the end, that the difficulty becomes political. (4) In order to start a practical system of reorganized priorities regarding the earth to work, it is first of all necessary to make this conceptual commitment complete, immediate, and existential, i.e., (5) the pet gopher sleeps with me when I go to bed, eats with me when I dine, walks around the house with me when I pace the floor; and just now, when I was in the bathroom crapping, she slipped in through a crack in the door and crapped. WHY THEN AM I NOT A GOPHER? The reason why I am not a gopher is because the gopher can wash up anywhere he goes, whereas I am confined to sinks in kitchens and bathrooms. (6) You fill in the analogies with plants; and thanks.

THE SANDHOG'S MONOLOGUE
In honor of the star-nosed mole

Is It at the center or the edge? Perhaps it's enough that I simply recognize Its presence, hanging there in front of my eye like a loose eyelash. But loose eyelashes don't mean much; following a night of regret, of twisting and turning, and elaborate psychic gyrations, it's easy enough to understand awakening and finding oneself a man with tousled eyelashes. But the Something was present all the following day; and last night It was also evident. The next morning, the same Presence, but a different analogy: It was as apparent as a Cuban gunboat steaming up the Potomac toward the Capitol. Curious, I said; but I'm not President, am I?; and I rolled over and went back to sleep. Later that same morning, at work, as I was attending to my molar labors, the speck in my eye continued to bother me, prominent now as a tombstone in a teacup. Perhaps I should say what my job is: everybody says I look like an intellectual but actually I'm some kind of sandhog. At the moment, I have a project over near the river: I'm trying to dig a tunnel between this city and the promised land just across the river, using only my bare hands and feet. Obviously if this Something of a Presence were real, I'd be among the first to be equipped to remove It. But the days go by and It grows still more ungraspable; and as time has gone on, I've become so used to It, I've even given up making up analogies for It. But It looks enough like an enormous boulder lying on my eye to turn my eye in on itself, and remind me how full of memories I am already. For example, I recall a passage from an astronomy textbook I once read in preparation for my vocation as an astrophysicist. It said, in its exquisitely scientific, professional prose: "When we look out into outer space, the optical evidence is that the Earth is situated unchangeably at the center of the Milky Way, the galaxy of which it is a part; and yet it is a physical fact that at this very moment the planet is moving rapidly across space to some other Galactic Universe. This new Universe is located just west of Cygnus the Swan; or, as it is sometimes called, the constellation of the Northern Cross." Is It at the center or the edge?

VISUAL EARS

Lying down in bed the other day I thought I felt something move somewhere around the left side of my head. It stirred in a stately way, with a definite and regular pulse — a little like Fred Astaire and Ginger Rogers in the waltz in the film version of *Top Hat* (1935). Then I realized it was only my left ear, through which blood was flowing in such a way as to rapidly increase and decrease the lobe size with each additional heartbeat I decided to take. Rolling over, I inspected to see if the impression of motion was occurring on the other side, too. Sure enough, it was. How excellent that the impression should have been symmetrical! This brings up the central problem of any true philosophy of hearing ears: Exactly how does one examine the possibilities of the human ear? Inspection usually involves observation, of course; but the only thing this ear examination has involved so far is feeling. Doubtless one could also listen to one ear with one's own other ear opposite it; or else both of one's outer ears with both of one's inner ears. Also there are the three related secondary questions: (a) whether all these ears are straining to hear the future, (b) whether this future will really be a better future, or (c) whether the ear is still in the earliest phase of trying to hear just what a future more satisfactory than the present one might actually be.

MOLAR ADVENT IN RETROSPECT

(1) Suddenly everyone is stricken by the pressing relevance of the courtly and hopelessly tentative love affairs taking place among five old orthodox Jewish ladies and five old practicing Catholic gentlemen, somewhere in a "non-sectarian" retirement community located just south of St. Augustine, Florida. (2) Also, at this very moment, there is someone in a Civilian Submarine at the bottom of the Gulf of Mexico whose actions affect us all with their secluded elegance; their secret grandeur, grace, and repose.

One thing at least that all men have in common: everybody knows that the standard life jacket worn by pilots and other military personnel whose service is at sea is called the "Mae West" model. The reason why is, of course, clear: it is hung just below the neck and it is inflatable to ten times the normal size. The standard naval life jacket received its name at the beginning of World War II, at the peak of Mae West's first popularity. But then after World War II Mae West lost her first popularity somewhat and gave way to other new rising stars such as, in the early 1950's, Marilyn Monroe. That was when I first discovered the so-called "Mae West Time Loop," and gave it its name. What happened is that when I first saw Marilyn Monroe in *Blackboard Jungle* (1955) I thought she reminded me of someone, only I couldn't remember who. Jean Harlow, perhaps? I wondered. But then I realized that the original model for the Red-Hot-Mama thing in Marilyn was not Jean Harlow, as everybody used to say, but Mae West. Another thing that tended to re-enforce this feeling was that at that time I had never seen a film featuring Jean Harlow. The final link of the loop was forged when the other evening I saw in a copy of *Movie Fun* magazine a picture of Mae West at the première of her new movie, *Myra Breckenridge* (1970). There she was, Mae West, looking familiar as ever, and I realized that it was not because Mae West was imitating the way Marilyn Monroe looked, which I had come to think of as being like that of Mae West, but rather that Mae West was looping back to looking like the original Mae West. To have skipped Marilyn Monroe entirely and to have gone back by a system of omissions to one's own origins — this is what is popularly known as the "Mae West Time Loop." God bless you, Goddess of the Screen now and forever, Mae West.

✿

(But no blessing is to be accepted from the goddess of plastic pollution: "May Waste.")

THE CAPTAIN'S KINDNESS
Or, NAVAL LORE

"Hey, what's that funny-looking coiled-up thing doing coming out from under your dress around the region of your stomach"? I asked my nice, novice pupil. "Oh my, I never noticed that before you pointed it out; that shows how much I depend on you for perceptions!" she exclaimed; "Tell me, what do you think it could possibly be?" "Didn't they teach you anything in G.S.E.C.; that is, Graduate School for the Emotionally Crippled?" I asked her. "I don't know," she said; "What do *you* think?" "*I* think," I said (avoiding her question), "that what that coil happens to be is the rubber band attaching you to the past. The way it works is you have to keep on pressing yourself forward into the future harder and harder to prevent it from springing back and snapping you back into the past with a terrible huffing and puffing sound, like that of a baby vacuum cleaner sucking its thumb. The curious thing about this system is that the harder you push, and the further into the future you propel yourself, the harder it is to continue for any length of time. And once it begins to pull you back into the past you'll never escape, it has the attractive strength of one of the currents that flow over the Gulf of Mexico, and that can carry a disabled motorless submarine from the Atlantic Ocean to the Pacific Ocean straight across the Isthmus of Panama without using the Panama Canal, as all the while the Captain clings to his periscope and the mates lie around on the floor of the vessel, dying laughing." At this point in my patient, reasonable explanation I notice the look of concern vanish from her face, and she stops tugging at that long shiny black thing coiling around her midriff. "Oh, Sir," she says, "I can feel it already; this life is going to be a pain in the ass; so may I cling to you for support; or to your periscope at least?" "No, you may not cling to me or my periscope," I say, "one of the things you don't know is that I've always wanted to be less like a Captain and more like the mates lying around on the floor of the vessel dying laughing. Still, child, although you may not cling to my periscope, I hereby agree to arise from my own depths for a moment and help you to cut your cord. (Else, be snapped back into the past with the unforgettable sound of tight garters coming off a recent corpse!)"

HOW A NAVY MAN GOES DOWN

"Old soldiers never die" — General Douglas MacArthur
(January 26, 1880–April 5, 1964)

He dreams of being surrounded by rushing sounds — it must be enemy aircraft on the attack. They go soaring around his head and buzz the brain, then one dives into his collar; it comes out through the starched cuff of his shirt. He waves his arms around wildly but one swoops up his pants leg and then comes out his fly that wasn't quite closed. What were the enemy aircraft doing beneath his clothing? Don't worry — they were only scout planes on a reconnaissance mission! Out of a cloud comes an entire squadron, blue as the sky, flying in perfect formation and buzzing like angry hornets: They break formation and one by one begin to dive down and in an instant they've torn the gold braid off his suit jacket and are gone again; then the Navy Man becomes aware of an aircraft carrier off in the distance, firing at his newly polished shoes . . . a scuba diver starts climbing up his left pants leg, he feels a little tug at his waist and notices his belt buckle is opening but before he can close it up again his pants fall down. Suddenly a blue helicopter is hovering overhead; it lets down four ropes with hooks at the end and, while he is staring down at his pants, they cunningly remove his service cap, as in guerilla warfare; then his regulation Navy hair flies off in the breeze and his false teeth fly out. Another helicopter appears: its four ropes lower to his shoulders, then as far as his wrists; and together, the eight hooks rip off his jacket. In the meantime, a team of underwater demolition experts undo the laces on his boots and pull his socks down; in an instant his new regulation T-shirt is burnt off by airborne flame throwers. "Oh, leave him his shorts at least!" a lady technician's voice calls out from a battleship that is advancing with all its guns firing. But then a squadron of pilots on a suicide mission arrives in the sky; one after another, despite his cries, they peel off from formation and dive their blue aircraft, aircraft blue as the infinite, down his throat; and one hears muffled internal explosions. Well, he's gone down now; but at least as the Navy's only ten-star admiral he had the right to choose his means of cremation, and to demonstrate that cremation and creation are actually the same. And as his scalp sinks slowly in the West, his devoted men, who are all poets at heart, give him a 22-gun salute — it's the salute reserved for the Navy's only ten-star admirals and their admirers; also, this salute is an honor reserved especially for distinguished fortune tellers, retiring jockeys, and female impersonators.

OF CHEWN FAT

Another aspect of post-Advent atmosphere: Across the street, a few feet before the picture window of a neighbor who uses language in a conventional way — without sensitivity to the danger of cliché or the literal truth of metaphor — there appear, as if by advent of Miracle, enormous piles of "chewed fat."

A CIVILIAN SUBMARINE????

Mole just refused point-blank to accept the slightest suggestion that he is simply a sort of "civilian submarine." But to have heard him refusing in his modest little voice it was necessary to have recited the poem "Molar Advent in Retrospect" in the first place, without being shouted down.

MOLECULAR MOTION

Also, somewhere near here, a mind must be moving freely through the tunnels of metaphor.

THE CATERPILLAR NEPHEW
Or, HOPPED

The old lady's lawyers wouldn't let any member of the family see the alleged nephew to whom Aunt Agatha left all her money. The lawyers kept insisting that it was only logical to keep him locked up in the antechamber. But once a week, on the day on which we would usually come to see dear Auntie when she was alive, and when we wanted to borrow money, we used to return to her room anyway and press our ears in chorus to the door. But the only thing our listening chorus could hear was the rustling of wings, and the scuttling of a lot of tiny footsteps across the floor — a floor which sounded as if it were littered with crumpled paper, but which was probably only our own money. So, reluctantly, abandoning ourselves to the joys of family nostalgia, we settled down patiently to wait for the death of our most recent relative — the mysterious favorite sole heir whom we simultaneously but affectionately began to refer to as THE CATERPILLAR NEPHEW. But alas, this touching story of contemporary American family life doesn't have a happy ending. One day we heard a scream: The nephew must have crept too close to the stove and burst into flames! So we all called for the lawyers. It was then that we noticed for the first time that although there were the same number of us, there were twice as many of the lawyers hanging around. And when they took us to Aunt Agatha's room, it was only to show us approximately five hundred cockroaches, running in every direction, mating and reproducing, with bits of Last Will and Testament in their mouths. Are these the true and logical heirs of the Caterpillar Nephew? We decide to ask the lawyers for more of their professional advice, and add: "Shall these be the ones to inherit the earth?" But are these legal people good for anything? Again there are twice as many lawyers as there were before, just standing around silently together in their multiplying numbers, mysteriously smiling in their high hip boots as the insects rustle restlessly at their feet; and all we can do is stare out at them from in here in the relative safety of an ancient Chinese armoire with glass doors into which we have recently HOPPED.

THE EXTRAVAGANT POCKET
Or, "CASH"

If Mole seems to be a sort of bookworm it's probably because of all the literature he finds in the garbage can. One day he reads in a thick text on politics and economics that perhaps the most characteristic of all human drives is towards the accumulation of something called "CASH." Mole understands all about "CASH": it's what acorns are to squirrels. On the other hand, squirrels only store up just enough to allow them to survive and maybe enjoy themselves a little, but Mole notes that human beings can go on collecting "CASH" forever, or at least until they die, so as to turn over what they have to others — the children whom human parents presume are going to be eternally grateful for their having wasted their lives collecting "CASH." Mole realizes that he himself is a collector, he collects worms, but still he likes to think that it's not for their public value but only for their beauty. Anyway, one day Mole reads that the human drive for "CASH" is intimately connected with the human psychic drive, the most basic tenet or aspect of which is the tendency to "safeguard the central self." Deep down in his multiple tunnel, the one that radiates as far as a mole can dig, Mole finds he can't take even the very first step towards following this particular train of thought. Their idea about saving the central self seems about as logical as the idea guiding a human being who notices that one of his pockets is inside out, but who then turns his other eight pockets inside out, too, so as to get a consistent suit. Another analogy that occurs to Mole is with a human being who strives to preserve the impression of unity by turning all his or her clothing outside in, except for the extravagant pocket.

IDEOLOGY MONEY?

In his book on Politics and Economics, Mole reads about "Gresham's Law," to the effect that "bad money" (defined as money insufficiently supported by collateral at the Mint) "tends to drive out or take the place of good money" (defined as money for which a sufficient amount is reposing at the depository). Looking over the earth from his own personal perspective (presently a drainpipe in a driveway) Mole finds that bad beliefs (defined as beliefs that people say they hold, but which lack the collateral of conviction) tend to drive out or take the place of good beliefs (defined as beliefs which people actually do hold, or at least actually can hold). Looking over the surrounding landscape from a molar viewpoint, it becomes apparent that around here bad beliefs have indeed long since driven out or taken the place of good beliefs; and that at present there is nothing on earth more destructive or dangerous to the idea of human values, than the idea of "Human Values."

ANSWER THE METAPHOR

A new number has just been set up by the Public Telephone Company, or the Department of Public Works, or something like that. It's for people who are interested in finding out What Reality Is. Naturally, when I hear about it, I ring up twice the first night and three times during the day. But the phone is always answered by some answering service, or by some metaphor of an operator. So now, answer the metaphor.

PROJECT FOR METAPHOR SCULPTURE

Like a poor old mother bird with an astonished look whose chicks have been snatched away by the farmer or grocer, leaving her a nestful of old egg-shell fragments; like a retired admiral who goes scuba-diving and while walking across the ocean floor comes upon the wrecks of former friends who were sunken sailors; like a street filled with the scraps of yesterday's newspapers; like confetti blowing in all directions after a parade, or like two thousand uncut diamonds in a mountain, the head contains the remnants of a day. In fact, it's exactly like that: there is no other way of phrasing that thought except through that metaphor. To see this particular metaphor better: construct a twelve-foot head from transparent plastic. It should be eight feet in diameter. Place it in a room 16′ by 10′ by 10′. Inside the head, stage an automobile accident: Two cars in a head-on collision, the drivers flung forward across the dashboards, through the window eyes, and out over the eyebrows and forehead hood. The pieces of the car and the bodies are suspended in mid-air from tiny invisible wires, fine as the tiny, nearly invisible hairs which curl around the neck of an actual mermaid.

WISE ADVICE FROM PAPA MOLE

All I remember about Papa Mole is that one day just after I was born, but shortly before he disappeared, he leaned over to me, cupped his claws, and whispered in my ear: "You know, sonny, don't you? — Mermaids are only a watery form of angels." Or maybe what he said was, "You know, sonny, don't you — Mermaids are actually angels, only somewhat more aquatic." Or maybe he just mumbled something about "aqueous angels." Anyway, though I forget the phrasing, and what he said certainly wasn't in verse, I understood the poetry anyway.

THE ANGELS
Or, GOD'S EYEBALL

The angels, the conventional angels of history, are coming to turn in their wings — a long line of identical pilgrims winds out of the warehouse where they are supposed to turn them in; the line stretches out in a straight line as far as that cliff over there in the distance; then the angel line comes down at an angle from the air, after slicing off from space. It's true that all these beatings of wings give the impression of taking off, but actually they're the sounds of vast numbers of seraphim wings hovering and landing for the last time. Inside the warehouse, despite the obvious fact that this turn-in represents a gesture of considerable philosophical gravity, feathers fill the air, and there is an atmosphere like that of a pillow fight in a dormitory for very young girls. After processing, the angels come out the other side of the warehouse (a structure which is best described by saying that it resembles God's eyeball); some are laughing and joking as if relieved, making supercilious remarks about nature and mankind and chatting casually about life in the fourth dimension where they hear they are going to be shipped to live from now on. The rest seem deflated and two-dimensional: they frown, look pale, carry attaché cases, pursue careers, act seriously, walk like mechanical men and women, and have keys coming out of their backs. Everybody seems slightly uncomfortable about these suits of new clothing they have been given to wear; and even now, so soon, they seem puzzled when they find the single long feather which has been placed in each suit for a souvenir. Also, as a second souvenir, everybody gets an indescribably beautiful and exciting plastic ashtray which is an exact replica in miniature of the warehouse; stamped on it in the silvery lettering angels are supposed to like are the words "God's Eyeball," together with the date of the present year.

THE CHURCH OF THE IMMACULATE PEANUT BRITTLE

"Hello, hello, is anybody home up there?" A voice straining in the night, coming from very near by. That's because it's probably mine! And also, there is an answer! A head appears at the window: "We're open all night all right, that's because this isn't a church anymore, we've been converted to a peanut-brittle factory." "But don't I recognize you, Sir — aren't you the former Sexton?" "Yes, after we were converted they thought it would be logical to retain some of the same personnel and so all of us agreed to stay on for a while." "Does that include God, too?" I shout up at the former Sexton. "Sure it does," the head says, and then disappears from the window. Then I see no head, or face, but I hear a somewhat deeper and more resonant voice: "My Son, my Son, we've been putting you on, my Son. But you know you should have come up anyway; you know it's true that for you, Christ has always seemed ideally suited for part-time work in peanut-brittle factories." "Oh My God!" — I say half out loud. Was He genuinely angry? On the way up the stairs to find out, I meet an angel whose face is covered with chocolate chip cheeks and licking his lips.

THE LOFTY LADY

Do you see that woman over here? Well, she's really *some lofty lady* — a kind of aging angel. You can tell how angelic and sensitive she is because every third thing you say to her either upsets her or insults her. You can tell about that because she keeps getting this look in her eye, glaring angrily around the room, in the meantime inflating her feathers like a crazed owl. What makes her angriest of all now is mistakes in grammar — or sppelingg. Oh sure, I agree: maybe she's not the cheeriest or most healthy creature in the world to have at a carefree New Year's party like this one — in fact she's not invited out too often anymore, except for business purposes — but she does help the time pass when things start getting boring by keeping things intriguing. In fact, she's *so* intriguing, she helps the time pass so well, that by the time midnight strikes you'll feel somehow that you're not one year but two years into the future. Oops, there goes the lofty lady again: she's been chatting with that little man in the bowler hat sitting on the edge of the couch over there; apparently he's just said something she doesn't care for, because look! — now suddenly she's twice her normal size, with burning eyes, and there she goes! — now she's pulled his hat down over his forehead and is putting her fists through the upholstery. Suddenly my living room is filled with ruffled feathers! The settee's and the lady's have become mixed, creating this great new lofty fabulous incredible aerial creature! *Look how she still can fly!* — Oh, pardon me, I'm a little high myself. But after all, it's Christmas Eve, isn't it? Well, anyway, now you can see why I invited her to the party, right? . . . Listen, here's a little friendly advice on how to start up a conversation with her. By the time she gets around to you she'll have become so touchy about *faux pas* and manners and linguistics that to keep her calm you'll have to pause after every sentence and tell her where the accents ought to be, also reminding her that you're crossing every "i" and dotting every "t" you speak. Also, you'd better put on this old suit of armor here, okay? Believe me, the ideal conversational style with a person like that is to enunciate very slowly, jumping back after every other word! Pardon me for shouting . . . But it's New Year's Eve again, isn't it? Oh, look, now she's signalling for an ashtray, she must want to smoke. Only everybody but me is pretending not to see her; I guess she's so intriguing that nobody wants to run the risk of coming into range anymore! And there she goes now! Now her delicately ash-pale face is red and swollen with rage and her veins are popping out all over her face and body just to show what a sensitive lady she is! Now the crazed owl with the ruffled feathers is tearing up the floorboard with her beak! *Oh, what a lofty, lofty lady!* Listen, since I can't walk so well any more and since the Easter Bunny is coming, would you mind, now that I've explained all this to you, at least going out to the glassware store on the corner and buying an ashtray? Here's a dollar; but you'd better hurry. This lady is so lofty, so intriguing, and she helps the time to pass *so* well, that even if you run all the way to the corner and back, before you get back at least a decade will have passed. But before you go: Best of luck for 1913, and (hic!) Happy Days!

THE NEW CHRIST

The lady eight months pregnant entered the room in which everyone was carrying on in a gay way. Despite the fact that the room was very crowded with carousers and merrymakers, the bump of her unborn baby so altered the center of gravity in the party, that a wallflower who happened to be poised on the edge of the ledge ready to jump off because she had not mastered the art of conversation, and who was placing all her hope in her ability to fly, was sucked back into the room and landed on the lap of *some very famous former movie star!*

THE ENDS OF ERAS
Or, ON THE JET

On the jet, when the famous T.V. preacher travels first class, while the other ten touring representatives of the Christian Board of Missions travel in the back of the plane, "coach class," with me, this tells me it's the end of some era or other — probably the Christian one. Moreover, when I see the same T.V. preacher's high-toned old lady of a lofty wife standing on line at the duty-free airport store to buy their legal allotment of Scotch, it is the Decline of the West. And when this lofty lady grows pushy and tries to sneak in front of me on the line so as to get back to the plane in time to get a seat near the window, it's the death of the entire earth through atomic holocaust.

THE SECRET OF SCOTCH

Why do people like Scotch so much, anyway? And what is the celebrated "Secret of Scotch?" It's definitely one of our time's, and this life's, most insoluable mysteries! — it's as if a bottle with a rolled-up message in it (a message containing the Secret of Scotch) had been dropped into the first vatful of Scotch ever invented, and had remained drifting there, lost forever to the enthusiasms of habitual drinkers of Scotch. Certainly it's lost on me: I don't like Scotch myself, much. That's why I recently decided to devote myself to a period of concentrated research regarding it. One afternoon I arrived at London airport carrying fifteen different bottles of Scotch which I purchased at the duty-free liquor store at La-Guardia Field in New York City and which — since I did not have to pay any governmental taxes on them for either warfare or welfare — cost 25¢ each. My research begins just outside of Heathrow Airport, in a motel. I spend a full three days there, a complete long weekend, and by the third day I've explored the Secret of Scotch so much that on the plane back to LaGuardia Monday morning I spontaneously burst out into a round of "Folksongs from the Highlands" that I never remember learning. Since then, I've continued to explore the Secret of Scotch wherever I go; my quest has taken me over many lands and seas and climates and bottles; and people, all of whom assure me that they love Scotch. But now that I've come to the end of my life of devoted research on this subject, I must reluctantly conclude that they really can't possibly like Scotch either; it's just that a large proportion of the population of England and the United States consists of research teams. You might say that I have discovered that the Secret of Scotch is that there *is* no Secret of Scotch — except perhaps the secret that, all in all, Scotch doesn't taste so good. So next time, or next life, try buying Bourbon or just smoke your good old traditional grass; and get high looking at the sunsets from the windows of motels located convenient to two airports serving the two greatest English-speaking nations in the world!

"REALITY IS A GHETTO"

Certainly this long-standing physical poverty surrounds us but isn't this current psychological poverty equally present and pervasive? And unlike the other poverty, isn't this one present by general governmental consent? Doesn't everyone except Presidents recognize what state architecture is like? However, in the field overhead there stands a handsome structure — one which the charming farmer's daughter who fills it with smoke while home on vacation from college calls "The Institute for Transcendental Meditation"; and across the door of this outhouse, a young Mole scrawls his sole slogan: REALITY IS A GHETTO.

TAXIDERMY

A mole finds the subject of "taxidermy" a very delicate subject indeed. Before he stamps his foot and disappears down the Mole-hole, he announces, shouting: "Everybody knows that everything on earth will have to become more 'Open.' This of course includes poetry. And when poems are 'Open' enough, people may be able to fit inside of them more comfortably, as if inside the skin of some original and novel animal."

PORTABLE THOUGHTS

(1) Here we are lying back here in bed again, making up things. Don't we ever get out of here? Then suddenly I find myself out in the next room while you sleep, making tea for myself with no memory of having left bed. How did I get out here? By "here" what I mean is "here," sitting at the typewriter with a glass of steaming tea, typing out this poem. (2) How come I can move this way, with no memory of having left bed? And what is this half-composed poem doing under this type-writer roller anyway? (3) It must be that for the first time this morning, for a change, instead of events containing ideas, ideas seem to be containing events. For the first time this morning, thought seems to have become portable. (4) And now that we have arrived in this new conceptual locale, the first thing we have to do is fix it up here and there. Of course, we refuse to hire an interior decorator — and certainly we don't need an electrician to install the stereo: we can do it all by ourselves this way, simply by thinking. (5) Finally, some day: our first full-course dinner prepared in our own new home! But how long will it be before we can invite to the housewarming party our very dearest friends and all those whom we have ever really loved?

ON PAINTING THE BATHROOM WINDOW

I'm trying to get something done for a change, I'm trying to get away from this tattered stack of manuscripts. Enough concepts! What I want to do now is some household task, beginning by repainting the entire house, starting with the battered old window above the bathroom sink. One coat covers up all the old paint; but whenever I reach down with my brush to touch up the knife slashes and other broken places in the paint where the original wood is still showing, the paint is instantly absorbed into the wood. It's something about "fibre" — each time I paint over "fibre," the wood starts to drink up all my paint. My father the carpenter used to say that the wood was "thirsty"; and that, to satisfy its thirst, it needed a drink of paint resin. That's why I give the wood a second coat, then a third coat; and each time, while I'm waiting around between the coats for the thirsty wood to finish, I make myself a little something to sip, too. And sometimes I come back in time to see the original wood finishing up its drink — no longer acting like exhausted wood in an old family bathroom, and I can see it satisfying its thirst like an antelope with lowered head, leaning over some pool in a clearing, gratefully drinking, sip after silent sip.

505 B   MISS MABEL LOVE.   J.B.&Cº

THE PRIVATE EYE

The private eye just accepted the challenging assignment! — that is, solving the mystery of why inner and outer are frequently unconnected; of why the outside of things refuses to accept having things *in* it, while the inside of things refuses to permit itself to have things *on* it. After signalling for his faithful oriental chauffeur, Buddha, the private eye grabs his revolver and magnifying glass and is on his way. First destination for investigation: The Human Head. The car screeches to a halt in front of a lady with an unflattering hair style! It's actually from 1957! It actually is! The detective pulls out his magnifying glass and finds himself confronting his first problem: he sees nothing on the outside *or* the inside of the head. His first solution to all his problems is to break down there on the curbstone and cry. His faithful oriental servant Buddha helps him back into the calm of the car. Who is this detective anyway? Before we can get a closer look at his face, he throws his cloak back across his forehead, and drives off. Shortly afterwards, on the other side of town, a fast car pulls up with a screech of brakes in front of the human hand.

THE JOURNEY ACROSS YOUR THIGH

At last! The greatest of all explorations on earth! Our ten intrepid travelers set out across the vast expanse by traversing the narrowest section of the promontory. Confident, cheerful, chatting, they are moving spiritedly, and breathing easily despite the fact that they are heavily loaded down with jewels, rings, and other token trinkets in case of chance encounters with hostile or greedy natives. Now they pass out of sight over the distant, enormous horizon; and there is silence, except for an occasional ecstatic cry. But what *can* be going on now behind those hills? All you can hear all of a sudden is a lot of panting and hoarse and desperate breathing! Then there is a series of outraged gasps; and then the sound of struggle! Finally the leader of the expedition reappears. It's an eye, crawling in on all fours! "What happened?" we anxiously enquire; but all it can do is choke out a few words of feverish explanation through parched lips. "This eye's throat is dry," someone says " — it's obviously because its canteen of tears has been emptied." As for the eye itself, it has just fainted. Carefully, swaddled in its eyelid, we carry the exhausted eyeball back to safety, only to see it awake a few hours later in this apparent terminal which evidently it does not yet realize is only the base camp from which an entirely new set of still more perilous expeditions are about to set out.

TILE LIFE
Or, THE MODEL

(1) Before they were married, everybody said that it was very enjoyable to look at his wife-to-be. She was after all beautiful even for a model! That was in fact precisely why he originally worked out this way of spending entire nights looking at her without clothing. (2) Their marriage was perfectly logical. He began by establishing the field of vision of each of his looks. Each look was almost an exact square. The shapes varied from the geometrically impeccable only in that they were slightly imperfect at the upper left hand corner or else the upper right hand corner. This deviation was the result of his nose. (3) It is at a party that he begins to commence with the structure of their love. This is where he first encounters her. The first night, he accompanies her home; he is obsessed with laying the foundation. So the ceiling of his eyesight becomes the foundation. Then he drops curtain-walls down from around its edges. For extra security, he covers up everything in stucco. Once, he catches her standing at the picture window, staring out at the person next door, a gentleman neighbor! Finally, their relationship is cemented. (4) At the end of the first year of marriage she herself is one third covered by tiles. They celebrate the second year with the covering of the second third, the third with the third. Finally she is tiled all over by his looks; finally, after three years, when she is the completely perfect wife of his vision, he walks all over the floor, setting out decorative ironwork and chairs, to augment the general hothouse atmosphere. (5) He dreams one night that she has taken a lover. But in comparison with this palace of a place, what could another lover construct? A rent-controlled "studio" apartment on the Lower East Side? (6) Still, the next night, he has an even worse bad dream, dreaming that his bad dreams may be real. One day, when she seems to be daydreaming, he says to her: "A penny for your thoughts." With characteristic generosity, he pulls out his wallet. "I'm dreaming of your future happiness," she answers, "of some day being a piece of slate lying in the bottom of your garden, or the pebbled beach before your estate in Connecticut. Oh, do you think some day I may really compete with the Grand Canyon of Arizona, or Yosemite National Park?" He thinks he detects a note of irony in that, but he decides to leave well enough alone. (7) Still, his doubts continue to increase. One day, when she is asleep beneath all the tiles, he tiptoes overhead and lifts up one of the little squares. A flash of light comes out of her eyes! What was that? Can it really be a flashbulb? Looking across the room, he thinks he can see some other light he must have overlooked, coming out from

between the cracks among some tiles over in one corner. He tries to lift up one small tile to see beneath, but it won't come loose. Finally, he has to pry it up using a screwdriver. A blaze of light bursts forth! It's a hundred flashbulbs all going off at once! In her mind, it is midnight, and she is dreaming of posing on top of the Woolworth Building, nude except for a Band-Aid and a fringed headband like a G-string. "The Band-Aid was for modesty's sake," he tells himself; but it's just no good anymore.

LISTENING TO THE LINEN

What is the true nature of the bed? I spend a lot of time in bed performing research, research, always more research! I not only spend a lot of time in bed but spend it there conducting my research with as wide a spectrum of people as possible. I'm so good at getting in and out of a person's bedroom that sometimes in the morning when a lady wakes up and looks shocked to see me there, and asks me what I think I'm doing there in the morning lying right next to her, I have to make up an excuse. So I always tell them something they'll like; my favorite speech when challenged in the morning is: "O, dear lady, it's not what you think; nothing at all happened in this bed last night; I simply stepped into your bed overnight in order to listen to the linen." And then I bend over in order to demonstrate the sound of sheets rustling, and in the course of my demonstration I usually manage to run my earlobe *up and down over every creamy inch of their bodies!* I fool them so well that some of them don't even mind when I come back the next night — that's when I carry in a hearing aid to attach to the tips of their nipples or a megaphone to slip discreetly beneath their nightgowns. So this is the true nature of the bed: I thought it was for sleeping and for sex but it turns out that actually it's also the best place for doing sly things to ladies and tricking people. The proof is that I've been doing this for years and in all this time have never been thrown out of bed even once! Once I get in I get in to stay; except of course for leaving immediately, the instant I become bored. The reason why I can do all this is because I know what the true nature of the bed is; I know that if a lady lover says I'm a liar I can always switch my story from the one about listening to the linen to a promise of love at first sight or eternal love, etc.

OF MANUFACTURED PASSION

The place where most of the world's passion is manufactured is located somewhere in the no-man's land lying between the borderlines of what there is and what we think there is. During working hours, down at the passion factory, you can hear all kinds of grinding sounds, together with something furiously pumping. My first visit there was with a lady who said she understood the exact value of each of her sensations. To prove that, she had her body tattooed all over with replicas of paper money. The most sensitive and intimate parts were printed with the largest denominations. On her corns and calluses were the small bills and change. Even her dreams were manufactured: she dreamt regularly of going to bed in a huge four-poster shaped suspiciously like a gigantic cash register.

METERING

"Metering is not only becoming increasingly central to the orderly functioning of the modern economy, but is today increasingly beginning to penetrate the public philosophy. Indeed, metering must inevitably become increasingly widespread throughout society, as the methods and subjects of contemporary metering practice gradually grow more diverse." I read that first line in the textbook and then snapped it shut. But then I started to think about it: here in the United States of America we meter the mail by weight and you pay a lump sum for a city bus or train ride; but in England all domestic correspondence travels for fivepence and they calculate every inch of your train or bus mileage. And in France, this anomaly exists: the busses are metered, the trains aren't; and I forget about the mail. In Germany in 1931 they rediscovered the Goose Step, an ingenious method of metering the military footstep. I read somewhere that recently, in Spain, they have begun to meter Mother's Milk. The result is an entire generation of starved children, with bruised noses and startled expressions on their faces. What are things coming to? I just remember that the other day I was in Italy, sitting on a couch with both hands inside the blouse bosom of my girlfriend's best friend, when suddenly I felt something hard. "What's that?" I asked, making light conversation. "I sincerely hope it isn't a malignant tumor!" "No," she smiled back, "don't worry; it's a meter. This is known throughout Italy, especially in southern Italy, as a Feel-o-meter. Don't tell me, Signore, they don't have them in your country!" she added. "Oh yes, certainly," I said, "that explains all those ladies jumping back when you try to kiss them in secret," I said. "Tell me," I added, "here in Italy, do you pay with a coin or a token?" "Coin," she said, stretching out on the couch. "But where is the slot," I asked. She cast her eyes down to the ground, then looked up: "Silly boy," she said, "sometimes I think you really don't know even the very first thing about metering."

THE MUCH-VAUNTED ELSA

(1) Hey, by the way, how come Elsa fucks so much — it's not that you'll catch me complaining! It's just that I'm curious to know how come? Can she really be that passionate and free, or is the rumor true that it's all just a hangover from her days at Vassar; I hear she studied the theory of economy there, and now she hates to let a day go by in which her birth control pill is wasted. "These things are expensive!" she tells you in a proud voice, as she gulps one down with a glass of Piper Heidsieck imported champagne and drags you off into the closet. Is fucking then not a matter of feelings for her, but just another form of emotional capitalism? Are my feelings just a plaything of the rich or a plaything of the poor? It does seem as if Elsa were counting everything — she has suspicious little "X's" all over her wall calendar and if you make it with her twice in one night she informs you haughtily that she "regards you as redundant." And how come Elsa is so free that every time I see her at a party she always goes around proudly introducing anybody she happens to be with as the person she is in love with or is living with. What finally told me just what she was up to was one night when I made it up to her apartment because I heard it might be private and I became carried away; and after a few hours of eternal love on tiptoe, I went into the bathroom and saw that instead of having cute "his" and "hers" towels on the wall like the old-fashioned housewives she hates, she has a sign over the john that says "Foreplay for Freaks." Oh shit; Elsa, alas! (2) No, there is no way around it; obviously, for Elsa, having sex is just one more form of accumulation; alas, it might as well be an accumulation of cash. Since everyone is so convinced about her reputation for being a great lover, it is clear that Elsa is a person who operates strictly according to the laws of conspicuous consumption. (3) Believe me, if she ever pays you the celebrated compliment of getting into bed with you, you'll receive the distinct impression as she is separating her legs that she's opening up a bank vault. (4) And in the end, I prophesy that some day all the multitude of lovers she goes around announcing will some day suffer a miraculous conversion, will wonder if the so-called "much-vaunted Elsa" shouldn't really be called "THE MUCH-VAULTED ELSA."

ADDRESS TO THE WOMEN OF THE EARTH

Women of the Earth! Some remarks regarding your destiny for a second! The famous fact notwithstanding that your body is good at containing things, whoever told you that your shape is not only a physical feature but also an intellectual fate? Women of the Earth, when are you going to stop insisting on filling yourselves all the time, when are you going to try fulfilling yourselves for a change? The way it is now, if it isn't one thing inside of you it's another, if it's not somebody's child you have in there it's somebody's cock. No wonder Mick Jagger can't get no satisfaction! Also, I'm tired of going to parties where everybody is supposed to be so free except that all these sad creatures do is go around desperately sticking their tits into you, or else "modestly" introducing you to the people they happen to be living with or sleeping with, through a megaphone. Women of the Earth, at this rate, for your liberation's sake, even husbands would be healthier! Women of the Earth, you know you're not a bunch of old hens sitting on a bunch of old eggs, good men don't only want to sit on you and are not meant to be sat on! Women of the Earth, tell me where did you ever get the idea that fucking is for a function, that cunts are instruments, that your bodies are for keeping you company, and that ladies are supposed to be lonelier than anybody? Janis Joplin, I love you just as much as I love Mick Jagger, but I think you're overdoing it already! Women of the Earth, stop using those snatches to snatch at people with! Women of the Earth, what are you doing with all this functional and boring fucking; it's a miracle — you're beginning to make the Virgin Mary look like a winner, with her curious concern for conception through the ear and other unusual aural sexual habits. So why don't we all try getting into bed next time and doing it with our ears, anything would be better than this, just as anything would be better for you than what you're doing to yourselves now! Oh Women of the Earth, OPEN UP THOSE ORIFICES! Women of the Earth, when will you fulfill yourselves, when will you free yourselves, when will you free me; when will you Women of the Earth become — ah! — Women of the World?

Madison Square Garden, December 22, 1969
In Mem. Janis Joplin (January 19, 1943 — October 4, 1970)

LAZINESS OR LOVE?

Ah, a great love at last! — A love one doesn't wish to leave. Or is it just that, lying down on one's back in bed this way, one's nose is pointed so that it seems to block off the doorway? In this state, a single eyelash prevents a potential exit by way of the skylight.

HOW TO MAKE LOVE TO AN OLDER WOMAN

Older women are supposed to be more experienced than everybody else is in matters of passion; but I really didn't expect what just happened to me to happen. Here is exactly what I found out about making love to an older woman. First she takes you to the foot of a big elm tree. She reaches into the lower branches and disentangles a long silk rope ladder. Then she tells you to climb into her treehouse, and to "take care." Then, pulling out a tiny lace handkerchief to signal with, a handkerchief embroidered with a needlepoint picture of "Sally," the chief performing electric eel at the Barnum and Bailey Circus, she begins to signal to a passing dirigible. Then, while it hovers overhead, you and this experienced lady climb in. Then she gives you the best private oral instructions on how to drive a dirigible you have ever had, while exciting herself surreptitiously by shuffling through a private collection of irresistible French postcards picturing Japanese-manufactured steam-shovels painted all colors of the rainbow. The crew, of course, keeps discreetly out of sight. Fortunately, too; because the next thing you know she is standing in the captain's chair nude from the waist up, and also from the waist down. And then . . . and then . . . (I can hardly bring myself to say it, it's so exciting) she puts on *a transparent lace hoopskirt over a suit of rusty armor!* To you, she offers a sort of dunce-cap with a half-moon on it, and a magic wand. And then, while the dirigible goes careening crazily through the stratosphere, with her pet monkey at the controls, she increases the level of excitement by showing you several of the original Mickey Mouse cartoons, dating from around 1937. To add even a little more "atmosphere," as she calls it, she shows them using a child's toy projector with a battery-powered bulb but worked by a crank. What happens next, when the movies are over, shows the most experience of all! When she says something friendly regarding moles, you find you are both unable to contain yourselves! You jump straight into bed, and there you spend some more time doing still other stranger things to one another.

WHISPERS FROM OMAR THE TENTMAKER
Or, SHINING SKIN

(1) Oh, a face clear as the clearest water. Then I drop the pebble of a single sentence above her forehead, and watch the ripples of my ideas disappearing in her eyes. (2) And now, along the length of your currents, sinking more deeply in these slow waters, I feel I am almost an appropriate guest. Already we wish we could turn, and view the whole world from within the beloved's shining skin. (3) But we do not deceive ourselves that this feeling will end, and we shall be as a standing pool, on the verge of being declared a "health menace" by the New York City Department of Public Pest Control. (4) And when this is enough of a nuisance even to ourselves, the sad song will come. But will it be a sufficient song to offset our regrets about having drifted here in the first place? Surely you have noticed how eavesdroppers make the most skillful whisperers? (5) Desirée, I sing to you now of the strange yet not entirely tasteless relationship between spit and sperm.

THE DEPRIVED LOVER
Carpe Diem

(1) Don't I know you from somewhere, dear? A minute ago I thought you were the lady I finally got to meet who used to sit across from me every other Friday at noon for seven months at the local Chock Full O'Nuts; but now that I've come so much closer to you I don't know: I see that those aren't eyes, those are two newly hatched baby hummingbirds; those aren't ears, they are two spare fingers, #11 and #12, which you simply like to store in your hair; those aren't nostrils, they are two mine shafts drilled so that someone can conveniently plunder the rubies of your tongue and mouth; those aren't lips, they are italic signs among the lines of type which fall out when your mouth opens; and listen — the two baby hummingbirds are singing and beating their wings all night long! Besides that, that isn't a neck, that's an auto wreck; that isn't a collarbone, that's a chateau of ghosts; that isn't a lung, that's a foghorn for long-deserted shores — your bosoms are the horn and the nipples are the "start" buttons —; those aren't shoulders, those are French windows behind which a lonely stoned nun is wandering, caressing and undressing; those aren't even little fingers, those are stickpins for a poor man's tie. In fact, that isn't a body you've got there anymore, because the only thing that remains from the way it used to be during our great days at Chock Full O'Nuts is that you continue to be cut in half as if by the counter from the waist down. (2) And what a revelation regarding the happy days of our courtship, and the best dates of our relationship, when to tell me you have reached the peak of your passion, instead of crying out, you hand me a bowl of Chock Full O'Nuts' "Special Chicken Noodle Soup," a "Brownie," and a "Nutted Cheese Sandwich."

ESTHETIC NUPTIALS

I invited our favorite famous writer, who happens to be a distant friend, to our wedding. To celebrate, he gets high and cuts up the manuscript of one of his most famous love poems, using a paper punch; then he throws it all over us in our hotel room, like confetti. And everybody considers us just one more nice normal average couple when I tell them that we spent the first night of our love in a motel room crawling around on our hands and knees.

THE HEIGHT OF CHIVALRY

Also, he had what you might call a rather unique method of tipping his hat: meeting a lady he admired, he would bend forward from his ankles, leaning out at an angle, tilting over further and further, until finally he would collapse in a heap on the floor in front of her.

DYNAMITE DEW

Don't ask me, don't ask me; please don't ask me or I'll have to tell you. Now: since you've just asked me (I wonder why people always say I trick them into things?), here's an explanation of why I don't think we should move away and live here together in the country. The problem is the Dynamite Dew. Let us stroll around here together for a moment, dear, while I tell you the true story of Dynamite Dew. At dawn, here in the country, as soon as the sun begins to warm the earth, and as the mists begin to gently condense, they begin to form Dynamite Dew. Yes, it's true; all those famous photographs you see of plants in the morning in the country with little clear globules of humidity suspended from them, and taken by microscopic photography, are actually photographs of the Dynamite Dew. Even by four A.M., before the first light, when sunlight is expressed by faint hints alone, such as birdsong stirrings and gradually rising temperature, you can tell that the dew is forming. Fall to your knees right here on this path, for example; listen closely to these innocent-looking hollyhocks; and soon you'll feel little explosions against your ear. And that is the way it is all over these woods at this very moment! Transparent, shining, each delicate drop of dew, darling, is like a tiny hydrogen bomb. And these bombs are attached tightly to their plants with thicker links than you think, which is the result of combining mist with leaf paste. So each of these innocent-looking leaves of earth is actually potentially homicidal! Or worse, suicidal! It's as if in wartime some submarine were to send out frogmen to attach explosives to a nearby enemy submarine only the frogmen get lost and attach the explosives to their own submarine, then swim away and get lost again and return again to their own submarine, only to be blown to bits upon arrival. The only reason why the entire countryside around here doesn't explode every morning by Seven A.M. is because fortunately the wind comes and delicately detaches each drop of dew or else defuses it by evaporation. Otherwise, in the country, even the dew would be dangerous, made as it is out of the pure, hard, compact atomic crystal of which of course everything else is also composed — I refer to the earth, water, leaves, sky, buildings, highways, tulips, the universe, and your nose, which presses itself so eagerly against this bouquet of poetry for fresh information regarding the intensity of my love, and the living conditions which would be commensurate with it. And now, my dear, have I sufficiently explained why I do not believe we should go away to live alone together in the country?

FOR LESBIA:, Or MOLESTATION
For Bill Knott

Aha! this was the eye that you used to watch everything you ever saw with; this is the hand you used for picking things up; and these — O these things! — are the legs you used for the purposes of mobility. Also, here are the auxiliary legs, the feet, meant for balance; and as a means of keeping your shoes on your ten tiny toes. And also, here are the upper legs — thighs, so necessary in order for a person to have something to connect the pelvic region to the rest of the body with. And that's it! That's what it was all about! All those years you spent at parties surrounded by concentric circles of men, while women with exactly the same set of parts, only ones that didn't look quite so good, spent entire evenings sitting in the corner sucking their thumbs. How amazing it seems now that it didn't seem to matter much then that you weren't terribly amusing, and that you were so uncertain of anything pertaining to your own inwardness or feelings that if somebody picked you up at one of these parties and took you home you refused on principle to fuck unless he told you he loved you, needed you, or was a member of a minority group. And so it's come to this: here, under the earth at last, I CAN LOOK UNDER YOUR DRESS. I always wanted to know you better, and now, you'll see, I will; nothing will keep us apart anymore, not the satin, not the thick make-up covering you from head to foot, not the rosewood of the lid. But oh phooey on all this formaldahyde! Now I know for sure that they have inoculated you with formaldahyde, dear, just as once they must have inoculated you against having any real feelings. But onward against all obstacles! One statement they will never be able to make about Lemuel Mole in his epitaph is that he preferred Masochism to Necrophilia.

LINES WRITTEN "IN DEJECTION"
In Mem. S.T.C.

She's dead now, the famous ancient debutante, Miss Linda-Lou Dejection III is dead. Here, now, finally, at last, all her most precious and most favorite secrets are really completely revealed! Just look at how little it took to make Miss Dejection so appealing! Namely, an inside of the body, and an outside of the body. But what was it exactly that made up all that beauty? Now at last we may make a little personal breakdown! What everyone must have admired is her narrow waist, and these slender hands; the generousness of these breasts; an exquisite little finger two inches long as well as 150 yards of small and large intestine. But in retrospect, was that really any better than having two yards of small intestine and a little finger 150 feet long? Or 150 feet of small intestine and a little finger two yards long? Or a generous waist and an exquisite bosom? It's harder to tell than I thought it would be; for once she was Queen of All the Garden Parties in Scarsdale, but now here she is, an ill-defined underground mass. Ugh, what the hell is all this mess anyway? I can hardly bear to put my paw into it to get the worms out! Goodness, what an excuse for an entire lifetime! . . . How did she get down here? It is possible that somebody else was as bored with her beauty when she was alive as I am now; is that how she made her way down here, beneath the rhododendron bushes? . . . No, it can't be, I know I'm forgetting what all these people who live above me pretend to believe. It said in a thick book of Plato with some pages ripped out that I found once underneath an outhouse that man is not only a creature of physical surfaces, but also he exists in his preferences and prejudices, his faith and his beliefs, his values, and the breadth of his humanity; in his dreams; and in the lofty visions of his art . . .

THE TWIN CITIES

THE TWIN CITIES, A LIST: Minneapolis and St. Paul, Buda and Pest, Serbo and Croatia. Also, there is the Kingdom of Fucking and the Kingdom of Perversion. "Oh! I beg your pardon — that's a mistake isn't it? I always thought that the Kingdom of Perversion was at best a tiny city, just a suburb of the Kingdom of Fucking. At least, that's what we learned in school during geography lessons. Just how large is it as the crow flies?" Sorry, the crow doesn't fly there; no animal flies there; only people fly there. And besides, you don't measure it in miles, you measure it in refreshingly original concepts. At the moment, all I can tell you about this metropolis is that at the center of the town square is this dream of making love to a gorgeous underage child midget's corpse with a limp while lying upsidedown in a sleeping bag.

OF FALLING DEEPLY INTO LOVE
Or, DIRTY OLD MOLE

(1) For Mole, falling in love really must have meant falling. For a long time afterwards he would arrive at wedding parties out of breath and with a concerned look, squeaking at the guests of honor: "Whee! Wonderful! Terrific! — but next time try and make sure that you really like the person you're supposed to love!" (2) The most incredible part of the cherubic child's letter to Mole was the part suggesting that they ought to see each other and make love right away, to prevent their passion from "becoming a memory." Is it possible, Mole wonders, that the solution to the problem of human feeling really is just one more version of the old Horatio Alger story, reinterpreted so that instead of suggesting that financial success occurs when man pulls himself up by his bootstrap, emotional success occurs when potential lovers pull themselves together by means of a jockstrap? (3) Mole, mole, what is it that makes you so filthy today, anyway? "Oh, that's simple," Mole says, "It's been part of my basic metaphor from the very beginning; it comes, naturally, from living — unlike you — an entire life on the dust and dirt of real earth."

PHYSICAL LOVE

(1) Everybody knows that, whenever true lovers encounter, the last thing it is, is mechanical. Nothing is a thing. It is so direct, so physical, the pressure is so specific, that when one part of one lover rubs against the other, if it rubs with any strength, the other part actually falls off. It falls to the floor; and among true lovers, nobody moves to sweep it underneath the rug. Delicate, radiant, and palpitating, as the relationship continues, more and more pieces come to lie there beneath the rug. Also, they lie there beneath tables, chairs, and (especially) couches in the doctor's waiting room. Oh, as everybody knows, all true lovers are only too happy to accept making love in littered rooms! (2) That must be why all true lovers will always notice — not because of lechery, but because of all the pieces falling off — how increasingly rounded any other lover seems. (3) But is there no distinction then between the most delicate abrasions, irritations, and touching; and hitting something? — Is all this making love just one more version of beating somebody up, of slapping somebody in the face, or cutting off parts of each other's bodies with knives? (4) I myself have often felt whittled to approximately the size of a pair of tennis balls or handballs. (5) At least, in any case, all true lovers must accept the fact that when they leave each other for good, they will not be able to leave each other the same as when they found them.

THE BEWITCHED LOVER

What happened here to my famous impeccable sense of proportion? That's what love is supposed to be, isn't it? — you're supposed to lose it. That's why only yesterday morning I ran to the window and threw up the sash because I thought I heard Santa Claus up there on the roof, I thought it was Christmas! But that scraping sound was only some other animal out there on the lawn chewing on something; or a rusty razor running lightly across my cheek. That's what it's like to be in love: when you swallow, I think it's the monsoon season in Thailand; when your eyelashes flicker, I dream that you are sweeping out the entire house. And when I see your ear in the midst of your hair, I dream I am sifting my vision through dark curtains, catching glimpses of *a certain nude lady*. Oh, your footstep as you go to work every day beneath my window is like the distant sound of thunder in someone's underwear! And whenever you carry me away, it is as if you were bringing me something! Oh come to me, true beloved, so that you can go away in a hurry again! Oh go away again, so I can dream you are coming back to me! But remember, because of your bewitching quality, when you come to me I dream you are leaving; and when you depart for good, the lover truly bewitched becomes certain that you are extending the possibilities of Eternal Love.

REVISE THE ROSE

> "J'inventerai pour toi la rose." — Louis Aragon

Now, build a metaphorical sculpture for the lovers who liked each other as much as they loved each other. And for these real feelings, revise the rose: unroll a hundred yards of red baize cloth and spread it out flat for the petals; and for the dew, for the indelicate dew that can burst the ears with the explosions of its evaporation, make sure that the long red cloth is strewn with big white basketballs.

"I COULD EAT YOU RIGHT UP!"

> For some sweet baby

She drinks your heart out with a straw. Then she places her cold spoon on your liver. She puts on a chef's hat and makes passes at your genitals with a spatula, all the while making flipping motions with her frying pan. Then she sends you to the stockyards to "join the club," as she says to refer to your being clubbed; but first she offers you a shock-absorber for your underwear! And that's when she takes you in! — her gesture of kindliness and solicitude as she offers you the shock-absorber brings the tears of joy to your bandaged eyes.

THE PAIN-ALARM

The Reality Manufacturing Company is proud to announce its latest, finest, and probably destined to be most popular product: the "Pain-Alarm" (© 1970). It was developed because, as millions of Americans who own ordinary alarm clocks already know, it is the custom of companies like General Electric, Bulova, Benrus, and Waltham to invariably equip their popular alarm-clock models with the noisiest, ugliest, nastiest, and most violent alarms possible. The "Pain-Alarm" (© 1970) is designed specifically to supplant this central tendency in American alarm-clock manufacture. Recognizing that where there is a preference there is a principle, the people at "Reality" have designed this new kind of clock for those who are determined that their first impression of every day, which is apt to be the one which sets the tone of the entire day, be disgusting and painful. It has also been the recognition of the engineers at Reality that although this agony is traditionally transmitted by ear, it is not necessary in our modern era that this impression be restricted to aural form. Thus, instead of waking you up with, say, the sound of somebody giving you the Bronx cheer from your own bed, or the sound of a radio exploding with mariachi music at 5 A.M. at the noise level of dynamite blasting out the first excavation in a rock quarry, this deluxe model offers the owner a still richer, rewarding, and more fulfilling everyday public experience. Each "Pain-Alarm" (© 1970) is furnished with a pair of boxing gloves mounted on fists attached to two steel accordeon "expanso"-rods which come out of two sliding panels on either side of the "Pain-Alarm" (© 1970). When it is time to awaken, instead of an alarm sounding, these sliding panels draw back and out pop the boxing gloves and they begin to punch you over the head as hard as they can — *as hard as you could ever hope to hit yourself!* While this is going on, this deluxe model "Pain-Alarm" (© 1970) hisses nasty things about your mother's character, implies that your father is a swine, makes you paranoic about your friends, and announces that your uncle makes love with inanimate objects. And what is the price of the "Pain-Alarm" (© 1970)? The "Pain-Alarm" (© 1970) sells for slightly more than the alarm clocks of the past; but those who recognize bargains in a time of revolutionary inflation will recognize in this product *its real value!*

DOSSIER OF THE TORTURER

In with the big stack of advertisements for Pain, Mole finds two interesting books of differing sizes. They are useful books, too. One is a catalogue of the ways people have of making each other miserable. It is entitled *Dossier of the Torturer.* It is so full of "human" needs and requirements, so full of "demands" made of others — not to mention the techniques of extraction and pressure — so big and thick, that Mole finds it useful as a floorboard for one whole room in the Mole-hole. The other volume is also a catalogue, this one describing the ways people have of bringing joy to others or to themselves. The cover identifies it as a "sexual manual." Examining this book, Mole notes that in contrast to the primitive simplicity of the most effective methods of torture, most of the methods of pleasure are so complicated and sophisticated that there is at least one place in the world where each of them is considered "perverse." But what finally convinces Mole of the rarity of joy and the prevalence of pain among people, is the very next day, when he finally finds a use for this handbook: it is so fragile, so thin, that he decides to use it to trim his initial adolescent whiskers with; but then, on the very first stroke, he cuts himself shaving.

ADAM AND HIS CELEBRATED CURSE
Or, WONDERING MOLE

(1) A mole begins to wonder: of course he knows that Adam's celebrated "curse" wasn't a curse at all; of course he knows that, in fact, any curse which involves the elaboration of self-knowledge ought to be celebrated indeed. Also, of course, it seems to a mole that it is in fact to Adam's credit that he sought out the apple of knowledge, even if the result was being expelled from Eden, where apples fell from above without trees needing to be shaken, and a living could be collected without effort. After all, what could be better than a situation in which a man, or any individual, is responsible for his own survival? (2) The next night, at an orgy sponsored by The Society of New Theologians, Mole expresses these revolutionary (for him) sentiments. A little drunk, and very high, he even pounds on the table to make his point! Finally, bored, one of the bearded old New Theologians leans over to pious young Mole and insidiously asks: "But what if, despite this angry philosophy, Adam's Curse is still with us, not of course expressed in the fact that man has to make his living himself today, which is after all in a mechanical age relatively easy; but rather in the fact that despite this ease, many men continue to feel the need for struggle, effort, exertion, conflict, toil, and pain?" From their comfortable vantage point atop an especially docile girl, but pitilessly, the four old New Theologians continue in chorus: "And not only that, but what if this celebrated curse is passed on intact among those who believe with the traditionalists that the value of a life is to be determined by its proximity to pain, i.e., to those who have accepted the apple of knowledge, yet who refuse to consume the apple of self-knowledge — the one sold at the fancy Neo-Freudian Viennese Bakery around the corner, in the form of a tart." A mole continues to wonder.

THE POWER PEOPLE

First but not last encounter with the Power People: At the funeral of a great 20th-century Socialist thinker whom, for his purity, you try to honor. A revolutionary for 70 years! — tears flow like evening rain. But where are they coming from? From you, from the mole again. Then the disciples of the deceased begin arriving. They are mostly relatively young people, all in their 50's and 60's. After doffing their workmen's caps, they begin filing slowly before the casket. But then suddenly one of the younger disciples has jumped on top of the casket and is shouting and pointing down! He's pointing to the coins over the dead man's eyes, and yelling that he always knew the old man was a dirty capitalist sellout! But in the back of the room sits a row of actual capitalists, all wearing top hats, striped pants, and white ties, and tails. "What about them?" I ask the disciple. "Oh, I can respect *them*," the disciple says, "at least they are what they pretend to be, at least they are honest about their ideas; and you'll see, some day we'll be powerful enough to make a deal with them." That night, innocent adolescent Mole goes home and rolls the first stone over the mouth of his burrow; and over the stone he writes the first of his radical political graffiti: THE ONLY REAL IDEOLOGICAL PURITY CON-SISTS OF HAVING A LOT OF IDEAS, ESPECIALLY ABOUT THE IDEA OF IDEOLOGICAL PURITY.

TALKING BACK TO THE LOUDSPEAKER

"Get up off your asses and make a revolution! Get up off your asses and make a revolution!" That's no empty slogan the loudspeaker has there for a change, too, Mole notes; the loudspeaker means exactly what it says, for once. Namely, that it is difficult to make a revolution while seated. Already, Mole understands enough about revolution to know that it is made while people are standing; in fact, most often, running. The point that the loudspeaker must be making is that revolt is inconvenient. It says so in the little manual of revolution, too, as Mole understands it: traditionally, in revolution, you have to have a lot of big crowds with everybody pushing and shoving; just like picking apples off the trees in Eden, you get to loot for food; you get to sleep together in one big room with a lot of people you don't know; also, Mole gathers from the manual, when the biggest and loudest snorer there rolls over on you or takes up most of your sleeping space, you're not supposed to complain, for the sake of revolutionary ideological reasons. Also, he's apt to punch you. Well, that's logical, Mole notes; but then a mole begins to wonder again: if inconvenience is a necessity in revolution, how can you make a revolution if you're tired or in ill health? — After all, Mole still remembers his own delicate early childhood! Then Mole gets to the appendix of the little manual, which explains everything by saying that, even if you're crippled, you can still become a full-time revolutionary by standing around all day in a dark closet on one leg.

PORTABLE WAR

(1) There are people who are pressing to end this war and Mole considers himself one of them, having even by adolescence spent more than his share of time digging for peace; then later, actually digging peace; revising political manuals to include serious discussions of the process of Molarization, etc. Still, he tries not to forget that the pleasure he has begun to take in these activities ought not to amount to a delight in struggle for struggle's sake, or effort for effort's sake, those contemporary, immoral, evil, and decadent versions of Art for Art's sake. (2) For a mole, the sole struggle becomes to contradict faith in pain; he becomes convinced that, in war and out, hell on earth consists of depending for one's bliss purely on the reactions of those in opposition to one's position. (3) It becomes clear to a mole: there are people who say they are pressing to end the war, but whose pleasure in conflict suggests that they are in fact The War, have always been The War, will always be The War.

JUSTICE IS JUSTIFIED

(1) "Justice is justified, justified!" Justice *is* justified. Still, if there is one thing everybody Mole knows among the underground population will agree about, it's that there isn't enough justice on earth. So, since justice is obviously justified, how come? A mole begins to wonder if it isn't because, although justice is a righteous cause, so many justifiers of justice justifiably seem, so often, and to so many others, merely self-righteous. (2) Still, justice *is* justified. For a mole in his tunnel, there is enough justification for justice even in the fact that he can find a metaphorical justification for it: which is that obviously it's going to be impossible to communicate with someone who is just barely keeping his head above water about the possibility of carrying around the subterranean on one's own shoulders. (3) A mole even wonders whether justice isn't justified because there are reasons for it which eliminate any possibility of self-righteousness in connection with it. Except out of the most active impulses of self-interest, where did anyone ever get the idea that it is somehow important to the health of the earth that mankind (of all people) survive? A mole wonders: instead of depending on a self-righteous removal of self-interest, might not survival some day be the product of an expanded and intensified self-interest: an approach elevating trivial personal, national, or racial self-interest to self-interest on a global scale? (4) Justice *is* justified.

(1) Since justice is so justified, a mole wonders next — when political people insist on the need for "a lifetime of struggle" or a "full-time commitment" to some "irresistably just" cause — whether what this insistence on unending efforts might not indicate is the ineptness of these same political leaders in realizing these "irresistable" goals. (2) Or is there perhaps a motivation for political leadership besides the realization of actual political goals? (3) A mole is as suspicious of old cautionary phrases as he is of traditional political slogans; and for him, "Watch out he doesn't lead you to your death" becomes "Watch out he doesn't lead you to his death."

DISAPPROVAL AT CLOSE RANGE

What happens when the human body really just doesn't like itself? Well, you can punch yourself in the face any time you want to express quick, efficient disapproval; but if you decide to use a bow and an arrow you'll have to shoot at your feet. The other parts of the body are so close they are out of range; they might as well be lying a thousand feet under the ground in a desert on the opposite side of the earth. Of course, if you wanted to set up a complicated system of weights and pulleys, you might manage to attach the bow to the floor and put arrow after arrow through the periphery of your body somewhere. But it's a difficult thing to get working for you! The reason why it's so difficult is that when the body doesn't like itself you have to get used to a new kind of aiming. Instead of pointing the bow and arrow at something else, and shooting at it with them, you have to point yourself at the bow and arrow, and then hope for the best. The same remarks apply in essence to expressing disapproval through the use of a broadsword or other major weapons, such as a cannon, field artillery piece, or other howitzer. One additional large-scale weapon suitable for human consumption to let the human body know what you think of it is a guided missile, which efficiently reaches a man after coming a long distance to blow him up. But of course the disapproval it expresses is rather severe. Although the guided missile is a modern device reportedly developed for self-defense, its activity has at least the resultant annihilative effect of such relatively slow-working, primitive methods of expressing total disapproval as hanging, drowning, or poisoning. Fortunately, there is a happy medium among these various areas, involving neither inconvenience, complete extinction, nor outright impossibility. When all is said and done the best and handiest expresser of disapproval is apt to be small, such as the dagger or pistol, the latter sometimes referred to for obvious reasons as "the personal automatic." Their use is so flexible that you can actually gradate your expression of disapproval, its subtle range extending from stabbing or shooting a few critical holes in the body's edges, to slashing or blasting off everything until the only thing that remains is the hand that began the original assassination or surgery. Now, some of these considerations may seem rather recherché to the novice who wishes to express his or her disapproval — the novice who has just suddenly begun to express disapproval by mumbling a few words in the mirror while putting on make-up or shaving. But later on, he or she may progress still further to bombs, some of the possible mediums of the future in this category being the hydrogen bomb, the Molotov cocktail, or an outright declaration of war; still, for now, the best way to begin is by hitting the thumb with a hammer, or by running a finger or two through the home garbage disposal unit.

FURTHER IDEOLOGICAL STUDIES

(1) After further study, an older mole concludes that his chief difficulty with regard to the intellectual content of ideologically based belief, is that there *is* almost none. That is to say, although it is the nature of even a mole's mind to move, it is the deepest nature of any ideology to be static. Doesn't the loudspeaker itself make it clear that its ideas are extended best not by further consideration, not by speculative thought, but by action and persuasion? Even to a mole, it is clear that nothing is more antithetical to the activity of any intellect which expects to survive than constant reiteration without variation. (2) In the little handbook recently issued to explain the handbook of traditional revolution, a mole reads that, *traditionally,* the first act of any ideological politics that succeeds is the forbidding of further ideology. So, for a mole, it begins to appear that the so-called "intellectual fear" non-political thinkers have of political-political thinkers is nothing more than the instinctive suspicion one species of animal develops for another species which is attempting in every way to destroy itself.

A CENTURY OF PROGRESS

1880's: a mole reads in Oscar Wilde: "As for living, let our servants do that for us." For the 1980's, what Mole understands is that his ideological friend, who is intrigued by the idea of a lifetime of struggles, is graciously proposing: "As for living, let our parents' former servants do that for us."

THE GOVERNMENTAL FISH-FARM

From the air, it resembles an enormous fish. The shipping offices are in the fins and billing takes place in the tail. In order to maintain the fish motif as much as possible, a distinguished private architect was hired and now the metaphor is continued not only in the pattern of the over-all ground plan, but also in the office equipment, down to the fish-shaped typewriters, memo pads, paper clips, and pencils. The clerks sit at fish-shaped desks and, thanks to the good offices of a little-known employment agency catering to specialists, the clerks are also fish-shaped. So are the executives of the fish farm firm. The receptionist is a young fish who wants to star in the movies so she wears too much lipstick — too much especially in view of the fact that fish have no lips. Outside, through the great plate-glass institutional window, you can see the water creatures sporting in their tanks, cavorting, talking, and flipping spray into the air with their legs. This brings us around to an unfortunate situation prevailing at the fish-farm. Since it is the government which has set up this particular program, hiring the usual government-quality managerial personnel from among the local mental charity cases, there has been a slight oversight in that the only thing not shaped like fish are the fish. In fact, the creatures underwater in the outside tanks are the men; while the fish swim in schools throughout the rooms. However, as usual, the government is excellent in compensating for slight oversights in its policy; and instead of declaring war on its own installation and blowing it up as a possible approach — an approach seriously considered by some Secretary-in-a-State — has decided instead to simply turn up the air-conditioners to "Full-Humidity" in order to accommodate the needs of the workers! The only oddity that continues to haunt the Washingtonian Imagination is that the fish-clerks have been insisting for some mysterious reason that one day a week be a paid vacation, a "day of solemn memorial"; and that they have chosen as this day, Friday. This is about all I have to say about the "governmental fish-farm"; except that perhaps I was being too hard on our government — someone advised me the other day that perhaps I was the one making the error, that everything was exactly as it should be — the fish *were* in the tanks and men *were* at the typewriters — that the problem is mine, and can be traced to the trouble I have distinguishing between fish and men. And perhaps my advisor was correct, perhaps I was wrong about that; and also perhaps I was wrong about our government; so that with my particular intellectual, organizational, and observational qualifications, I now have every intention of applying soon for a job in the U.S. Civil Service.

RETURN TO ROOTS

Return to roots, return to roots! They're melting down the melting pot again, now no one's talking about living rooms anymore, now everybody's busy with kitchen imagery. A mole has roots of his own to find of course, but there is something about even this ideology of his own which makes him feel a little guilty. So he softens his voice a little: he remembers enough about history to remember that there has never been a wave of nationalism which hasn't tended to provoke a war; he remembers enough about the memory of popular historians to think with amusement that the only thing the statue of Garibaldi in the park means to most of the people in New York City is a big joke when the pigeons come to crap all over it.

GRASS ROOTS
Or, IN PRAISE OF PAINLESS CONTEMPORARY DENTISTRY

In order to truly understand a plant you have to remember that whenever something happens above the ground, such as a leaf, something is always happening underground, such as a root. A mole wonders whether Man can really achieve so lofty a thing as Vegetable Balance — much less be a tree. Certainly Man practices all the time — but mainly in his unconscious, by lying around nightly in the darkest places, feeling his tooth roots grow. Still, for true Vegetable Grace and Balance, a mole knows that there is nothing like taking a long lifetime's walk in the woods; a mole refuses to believe that you can learn to imitate the shrubs while in the suburbs. (2) The good thing about woods is that there, in the field, creatures are free to assume any kinds of roots they want; there, in the underbrush, one's thoughts can proliferate until they assume a life of their own, as long as they are flourishing ones; there, one can improvise from the invisible, to produce an individual foliage. (3) For the health of the roots of the future, a Molar Prayer is delivered from non-existent knees: "Oh, all you humans who are secretly envious of Vegetables: May your thoughts be so healthy as never to suffer future decay; and may you never have to take your plant for a visit to the dentist. But should your own thoughts not be sufficiently strong, you can always trust a contemporary dentist — for one thing you can always expect of any exponent of modern painless dentistry is that he will be a master of allegory."

A BOOMERANG-SHAPED BALD SPOT
Or, THE FALLEN MOUSTACHE

One good reason to *try altogether another moustache:* — For a while, on the advice of a skin man, I attempted to extend the boundaries of the present moustache. I let it grow longer, I altered its shape by taping it to my forehead; then I varnished it so that the hairs would cling together and finally I shaved it all off in one piece. It looked very good there in the ashtray on the coffee table, and as a centerpiece on the dining room table it made quite a provocative conversation piece. But then the cat got it, and ran off with it up a tree; so I guessed the logical solution was to try and grow another moustache altogether. The first variation I attempted was instinctive, if somewhat ominously childish; I slipped a pencil between my upper lip and my lower nose and walked around telling everybody what to do and screaming "Heil Hitler." Just think, only a few years ago, hair meant war! The second moustache substitute occurred after considerable meditation in opposition to the first. After much thought, I made a moustache by cutting it out of an old newspaper; but then, after a little more thought, I realized that like the first moustache this moustache wouldn't work for one very good reason: it wasn't fire-proof. Besides, when my cat went by again and I reached out for it, it didn't recognize me, and it squirmed and scratched my face. That was when I decided that something more radical would have to be done: so I took a book and stuck it on my face — then a piece of iron grillwork from the fireplace — then an old oil painting — then a set of antique shears. But the book wasn't good for reading any more at such close range; the sparks flew all over the room; the oil painting was a forgery; and the blade on the pair of antique shears rusted and looked too much like a rash on the human skin to remind anyone of a moustache. So I had a clock installed on my head but people kept staring at me to tell the time. Finally I decided to do what I usually do when faced with my particular set of everyday personal problems: I held a family council. And it was certainly good to see some of my relatives again, Sid with the box turtle in his hair, Phil with the perfect vacuum for a wife, Uncle Ed with the harp in his pants; and so forth. Finally, it was my trucker uncle, Uncle Salvatore, who gave a helpful hint that prevailed by popular vote, although I objected strenuously — that's why you see me here this afternoon, helpless on the highway among the gas-station attendants on coffee-breaks and other typical upstanding Americans coming down the road with my face attached to the front of a Mack truck and kicking and screaming.

"X"

Mole's political conscience flares up again when "X" is sent to jail for 333⅓ years for smoking ⅛ of a funny cigarette which in reality consisted of old ground-up Mother's Day cards that he himself had once sent to his very own Mom! A lot of men and moles are working now to get "X" out of jail sometime before the end of his sentence. And that's why it seems doubly unfortunate to hear that "X" is, by general consent of everyone who has known him personally, an absolute double-crossing opportunist, cad, nasty fellow, rotten guy, bore, boob, bum, and general head-fucker. But according to political and legal logic, this is precisely what makes him the correct man to defend under public law! Nonetheless, a mole wonders what it would be like if for once our leaders actually represented our heads; if their words were worthy of our ideas; and if all our slogans were poems.

THE RECENT PRESIDENTIAL ELECTIONS
Or, THE RETIREMENT OF A POLITICAL MOLE

(1) After the recent election, Mole sends a tear-stained telegram to all the "full-time revolutionaries" he knows, all the righteous ones committed to "a lifetime of struggle." He compliments them all on the ecological aspect of their accomplishment: after all, haven't they succeeded at last — after the failure of all previous efforts — in finally electing as President a genuine skunk? (2) Before withdrawing for good to his hole to meditate on the esthetics of politics, Mole scrawls the last of his political graffiti across the stone he has just rolled across his doorway; it says: DON'T TRUST ANYONE WITH AN I.Q. OF UNDER 130.

THE POLITICS OF METAPHOR

For a full-grown mole, the future has never begun to exist except as a form of thought; and thought has never begun to exist except as a form of language; and language has never begun to exist except as a form of metaphor. Even for a mole in his final circle of tunnels, there is always one more larger, more generous set of relevances into which all previous relevances fit.

THE TIMETABLE FOR REVOLUTION

After much deduction, finally, late one Christmas Day, a mole figures out an answer to that traditional holiday-season riddle; "Yes, Virginia, Angel," he answers, "there *is* a timetable for revolution. However, the initial entry is the requirement that, for absolute and immediate change on earth, first everybody presently on earth will have to be either indifferent to the present, or dead. Here comes the revolutionary express now, barrelling down the tracks of your present capabilities, covered with cobwebs!"

FINAL THINGS

In the end, Mole's political studies reveal this crucial and ultimate distinction between opposing Power People; he writes in his notebook, in his flourishing, post-adolescent hand: WIFE-BEATING A SURE SIGN OF DEPRAVITY AMONG CONSERVATIVES, GIRLFRIEND-ABUSE A SURE SIGN OF DEPRAVITY AMONG RADICALS.

THE LECTURE ON MOLIÈRE

One thing you can't say about Mole is that he fails to understand the true value of pride in roots. One day, just to show how much he knows he knows because of his own roots, Mole goes off to the local city university to deliver an impromptu lecture to the people on Jean-Baptiste Molière.

LOVERS AND LEVERS

Laughter from beyond the ground; Mole is much amused when he reads in the sexual manual that — notwithstanding the reputation of gardeners in D. H. Lawrence and warriors among Capitalists and Indians — primitive people make the worst lovers. Even his beloved Elsa-the-Groundhog reports that she was always disappointed! Some odd associations here that a mole's mind tries to bring together: one night he dreams of the differences between skilled and unskilled laborers, of the connections between levers and lovers, and the proper handling of tools . . .

It's another discussion on the motive for war. "I say it's economic exploitation," someone says, shouting from the first row of the political symposium, and into a microphone. "No, no, it's evil desires regarding oppression of underfed victims," someone else sensitively whispers into a bullhorn near a mole's ear. "No, no, it's Imperialism pure and simple," someone else asserts casually, firing a revolver in the general direction of Scarsdale and the other suburbs surrounding New York City towards the north. Now, here at the symposium, everybody is becoming excited; and the excitement is adding to the excitement! A mole has his usual reaction to excitement: boredom. By now, Mole refuses to find excitement exciting; once and for all, and for good, *it's Peace alone that interests a mole.* To keep himself awake during the debate, he whispers a few words into the ear of the Child-Angel who brought him to this meeting in the first place. "I just realized," he says; "what if the motive for war is the same as the impulses of these people exploding here; what if the motive for war is a feeling of boredom with peace? And what if, just as this struggle and aural torture is an instance of war on a domestic scale, war, with its explosions, is an instance of struggle and aural torture transported to an international scale? And what if delight in struggle of any kind is always expressive of failure to create a higher order of joy? — Tell me then, where would that leave an innocence that isn't interesting?" But there is no answer to Mole's question; and when he looks across from him he sees that the Angel is becoming drowsy because of his own machine-gun-like outbursts; that she is leaning over in her chair; and, in fact, has just fallen asleep.

THE THROW-UP CLUB

To show how free I was I decided to join the Throw-Up Club. The initiation was certainly exhausting. To introduce me to the way of life traditional to the Throw-Up Club, everybody kept showing me pictures of sections of the countryside before and after mankind got hold of it. The only areas that had been vastly improved were the parts formerly occupied by the estates of millionaires who once had the good sense to hire artists as advisors, such as sculptors, landscape architects, or poets. Then, when somebody told me that those were the same millionaire industrialists who were dumping junk all down and up the Hudson, that was the first time I came very close to throwing up; but then, in the end, no luck. My hopes rose however when I saw the club librarian pulling a dossier of U.S. Foreign Policy Statements 1963–1970 out of his briefcase. I must say, I did begin to gag and choke, and I heard a round of applause break out when I got up and ran to the sink and threw my head hard over the edge . . . but the applause died down when I fell silent and when, to get rid of my embarrassment, I pretended that I just wanted to pour myself a big glass of water from the tap. An hour later I grew even more embarrassed. The most gifted member of the club, the talented Mr. O'Fatso Blondelle, had already thrown up three times *just in the course of casual conversation;* and the thin individual they called Mister Skin-Bin had barfed all over himself no less than six times, while looking at a situation comedy on television called "Green Acres." The others were not so distinguished in terms of quantity, but excelled in general sensitivity. Among the ladies present, Hester-the-Pinwheel had thrown up just at the color of my socks and Marsha Arse did it while just sitting in the corner staring hard at nothing! The most sensitive of all was Herr Lazarus Von Udder, who, during our discussion of the ideal of "beauty" as it appears in Plato, kept sticking his head out of the window and showering the passers-by. And I couldn't even get a drop out when thinking about the poetry of Yvor Winters, or the esthetics of The New Critics! or even the dilemma of students studying new poetry under the tutelage of so-called men-of-letters who hate the idea of it! Finally, out of desperation and a desire for membership in this glorious fraternity, I resorted to the good old traditional trick of sticking two fingers five inches down my throat. "Foul, foul!" cried O'Fatso. The Bin was silently frowning; but Von Udder was livid! In the end, it was Marsha Arse who rose to my defense. "Look," she said, "we all understand that it wasn't the kind of impeccably pure act the rest of us have come to expect, the kind of action that shows that the course of our physical activities is guided by only our finest, highest, spiritual aspirations. Still," she continued encouragingly, "still, I think we should take his gesture under consideration, as a healthy step toward the kind of action which we require, and which is truly free, independent, and relevant. I call this meeting adjourned." There was a faint ripple of applause, and, looking slightly nauseous, everyone began to file out. Hester-the-Pinwheel had been silent all this time, but I guess she also was on my side: "Practice at home," she whispered as she went by. Then they were gone.

THE AGERATUM TRAGEDY #1

When we came back from the country I found my first and favorite ageratum lying down on its side. Was it tired? Its fluffy blue flower was beside the pot, and its stem, after coming out of the earth, lay over the edge. What are you doing down there little Ageratum I said in my most agreeable way, but it didn't move a muscle. Just then my best beloved came in with a glass of water and threw it on the fallen ageratum. At the touch of the very first drop, my ageratum brightened up considerably — unless it was my imagination. It's sad: all that remains now of the Ageratum Tragedy is a little scorched place around the rim of each of the lower or older leaves. The younger or higher leaves show not even the least sign of burning. Since then, so much time has passed: once my best beloved and I used to sit around together by the fire and weep to think of the joy, pain, and horror of it all; but no more.

THE AGERATUM TRAGEDY #2

Growing ageratums was turning out to be such fun that once I decided to try and grow more than my one precious previous one. So I threw a handful of seeds onto some wet flat earth in an old cigar box and waited. After ten days to two weeks, just as the seed envelope said, 157 little ageratums began peeping at me with their little blue eyes from over the edge of the soil. I decided to place them in the sun which comes in through the bathroom window, the sun which is the earliest and the brightest sun of the day. This was just like awarding some kind of medal to someone you love, I mused. But then, by using the toilet seat as a launching platform, one of my three dear cats jumped up onto the bathroom windowsill and knocked my cigarbox of 157 ageratums to the floor, so that the little rectangle of earth containing the 157 seeds broke into 777 little pieces. I was about to spend that day wandering around in a melancholy daze, perhaps composing several sensitive songs and poems about the Ageratum Tragedy, but then my best beloved suggested I do something constructive for a change, so I spent the entire evening sweeping up the fallen earth and sifting out tiny ageratum plants, which I then transplanted back into the cigar box, where they belonged. But still I was saddened that not only had the growth rate of the ageratums been upset, not only had several ageratum stems been broken off in the process, but 137 of the plants had become lost for all time in the cracks in the bathroom floor. The moral of ageratums is that although sometimes even tragic accidents have favorable chance outcomes, overtones, and ramifications, at other times there are none. Yes, unlike most other tragedies which have positive or at least diverse results, I decided that my Ageratum Tragedy was a true Tragedy, unlike most other tragedies or miscarriages of fate, serving no joyous purpose whatsoever.

INVASION OF THE INTIMATE PACHYDERMS

Elephants are attacking the roof of my mouth! Yes, beloved! That's why I don't have too much to say over the breakfast table this morning! I feel their tusks along my teeth and their ears brushing my gums. "How interesting! — How do your gums feel, dear?" You mean my palate? My palate, where I might actually taste something to enjoy it? I hope you mean my palate — the fact is, I don't feel like inviting anything there at all anymore. "Well, dear, numbness is another sure sign of elephants — you'd better go and brush your teeth; and don't forget to visit the Doctor." At the Doctor's: "Don't worry, Son; there's only one of them now, and it's only when you're lying here dead that I can commit myself to diagnose this as the first of a larger herd. But feel free to give me a call if you hear the sound of thundering hoofbeats or if you suddenly start spitting out elephant tails." Thank you, Doctor; I'm glad to hear that it's only something as simple as a single angry, trumpeting elephant in my mouth; and that everything's going to be fine until the next time I swallow. "That's a good point, Son; if something goes wrong we'll have to move fast! — That's why I've just decided to put you in the hospital for observation. Frankly, the way things are going, your first elephant tails could very well arrive within ten days to two weeks; you'll receive them either in your mouth or through the mails, wrapped in a plain brown envelope, which is the way Death, the famous pornographic zookeeper, sends things. And please remember, Son, we want your body for an autopsy." Doctor, Doctor, will I be able to visit my dear wife and mother one last time? "Yes, you will, Son, but she'll have to come and view the body here at the hospital; and please remember to limit your conversation to two or three words." But I know that won't be enough for her, she cares for me so much; and besides, I'll miss me so! "Now don't go around complaining, young man; you've obviously lived a full life, rich with love and concern; and as your mouth begins to fill with baby elephants, then mama elephants, then old papa bull elephants giving their mating calls, remember this: others have felt this way before you; and you *could* have been filled with hippos."

OF HOLES

(1) Bad night. Harder even to sleep than to think. Entire body clenched like teeth, omitting no finger, cell, or nail. At least, if these teeth were smiling . . . but no, this is a genuine grimace. It's the fault of the dark, it's the fault of the dark! — suddenly it fails to resemble one big single nice enormous nothingness, but instead resembles an endless series of emptinesses laid out end to end. Beside the bed, the holes of a harmonica look like the famous bottomless pits of the Mindanao Deep, in the Philippines. Nor, looking at the pores in your nose, are we spared the sight of the Black Hole of Calcutta. Either everything has now become empty, or else nothing needs to be filled, since everything here is crowded solid with these holes, vacuums, and tunnel-like spaces. (2) I fall asleep counting the edges of the emptiness as if they were sounds from the bells around the necks of the sheep I'm supposed to be counting. So this is supposed to be relaxing, this is supposed to put people to sleep? Oh, that's funny, very funny — notwithstanding the fact that I'm lying here frowning from head to foot. (3) And here, in the morning, beside the bed, is this sheet of paper covered with words, an effort no doubt to fill the empty spaces with some kind of sound. But if this is only a compromise vote for noise, there must be a better way; already I'm thinking that another way of voting would be to go out to the middle of the forest to invent a ballot box by shouting at the top of one's lungs into a hollow tree.

A HOPE CHEST IN REVERSE

For the sake of his continued "development" he was always shedding a new skin. Finally he had a chest full of them, a sort of hope chest in reverse. So in order to convince everyone of his continuing progress he held a celebration. At the party he came out wearing all these ancient diaphanous rags — of course he was trying to convince everyone of his philosophical advancement, but all he looked like was someone who had cut his entire body badly while shaving and who had covered himself with tissue paper from head to foot to stanch the flow of blood. His best friend, who happened to be present (and who also was later canonized for being a saint), said something kindly: he said he "resembled a pile of litter whose basket had been removed." His friend the Saint's girl-friend also cheered him up when she said that with his odd old garb and extensive and theatrical gestures of fare-well, he kept reminding her of the strips of paper they fasten in festoons to the vents of air-conditioners in Chinese restaurants in the summer to assure the patrons of the presence of fresh air.

OF MOLE'S BAD VISION IN CHINESE RESTAURANTS

Everybody was sitting around after dinner last night in The Chinese Restaurant, laughing, and reading the little slips of paper from the fortune cookies. People were reciting things like: Advice will be given to you well One may think what he dare not worth following. , speak. ,

and Habit, often mistaken for love. . Mole's fortune was a bit different from the kind everybody else was receiving, however. His little slip of paper read: "Oh Mr. Mole, Caucasian cousin of oriental sage, Mr. Moto; Oh, Mr. Mole, you who adore adding as much to your bodily weight as you can, and who consume twice your weight each day in food by eating twice a week at Chinese restaurants; Oh honorable Mr. Mole, consider this fact: the body is a most elaborately baroque exploration of space! Are there not parts that project like oblongs — I mean the fingers and feet; pyramids — I mean the thumb; disks — the ears; obelisks — nose and penis; and so forth? Such that the only generalization one can make about bodily shape is a non-geometric generalization; namely, *that there is no part of the body that is truly a part of the body that is not actually attached to it.* And yet, Mr. Mole, this is to be your fortune: sometime soon, due to hidden predators some of whom are lying here secretly within this very city, yet with whom you have no common ground — because of them, sometime very soon, you may soon be able to see *all sides and angles of one of your favorite bodily parts.*" As soon as he reads this, Mole slips the remainder of his dessert cookie into his pocket, crumbles up his remaining fortune cookies between his claws, and, mumbling something about a false formula for the future being worse than no formula for the future, exits. He leaves discreetly, however, by drilling a hole straight through the floor and down to the 103rd Street stop of the West Side IRT, in the basement. One of the sophisticated older girls in our party was skeptical: "Oh phooey," she said, "I bet he was just making it all up." As for me, I must admit: I'm puzzled also. I know Mole's vision isn't very good in the light, and wonder if "angels" wasn't just a misprint for "angels." Still, I find it difficult to imagine what the word "sides" might be a misprint for.

ON THE LOSS OF RAW FORM

There is no more raw form any more — If you want to get fat, you can only get it in the form of food; if you want shelter, you can only get it in the form of an apartment; if you want wealth, you can only get it in the form of money; if you want protection from the cold, you can only get it in the form of shelter. Things are that far gone! Also, in case you don't care about possessions, that is, in case you were thinking that feelings were what you needed: if it is somebody's opposition or enmity you want, you can only get it in the form of an insult or a scar; and if you want love you can only get it in the form of fucking. As for having lofty philosophical goals: if you want an immediate peace, it seems you can only get it in the form of fighting. But at least one thing is certain from all this: that in order to secure a lifetime of fulfillment, goodness, righteousness, happiness, and bliss, the most effective way to go about it is to start out by hitting your uncle directly across the face, while riding a bicycle, with a butterfly!

CALLING THE SUPER

We call the superintendent up to fix things, and he thinks he's doing it. But whenever I hear him banging at a needle valve with a monkey wrench, or prying the cap off a can of "Three-in-One Oil" with a crowbar, or hitting a sink pipe with his fist, or sawing off an inch of wood with a keg of T.N.T., it is clear as anything is ever clear that he has not so much come up here to fix what has been broken, as he has come to carry on one more campaign in the practical man's continuing war with matter. Clearly, our Super also needs to be repaired.

PRELUDE TO ANEMONES

I walk into my dark garage: it's filled with hundreds of flowering bulbs of some kind, the cases broken due to the inspirational force of the damp. It's true: it's not that the seeds want to come to life around here; this is happening because we have a garage that goes around pretending to be the ground.

PLANTING ANEMONES

Open the mailbox, take out the mail. But what's this? At last, it is fulfilled, my order for anemone seeds! Odd seeds: they aren't round as decent seeds should be; or even oval, or rectangular, or regular in any way. And they're much bigger than the average seed. No question about it: what they look like is *a bunch of fat nuts.* But no; these protuberances look just like ears. I recognize ears anywhere, whenever I see them. These ears are so big and obvious, in fact, that they make these seven seeds look like miniature models of the head of Mickey Mouse. So here I am planting seven brown models of Mickey Mouse in an earthenware pot and expecting to receive flowers, because at least I've seen pictures of what these seeds turn into in my *Encyclopaedia of Modern Gardening.* But what if my plants haven't read the *Encyclopaedia?* And what if I'm not equal to the genius of Walt Disney; what if his genius at transforming four mice, five ducks, a dog, a wolf and three little pigs into a fortune during the late 1930's Depression years isn't my particular genius at transformation? Oh, Disney was so pure he could even plant a girl named Snow White deep in sleep and have this maiden come up as money — though of course he had as his gardeners seven dwarfs, diligent and intelligent despite their rather peculiar individual sexual aberrations regarding sleeping young women . . . so that throughout the world, except at Walt Disney's studios, these sickly yet sophisticated gardener dwarfs are known as "The Persephones of Perversion." O Princess Persephone, queen of all growth above the ground, and mistress of all metaphor, grant this supplicating earthly seeker of symbols no common literary career, or even one in what is commonly known as show business, the film business, or any other business; but display for me a plain clear sea of red, blue, pink, and simple purple flowers.

OF KILLING ROACHES OR ONESELF WITH ONE'S WRIST
Or, HOW TO BE POPULAR

(1) Yes, of course, you'll say I shouldn't have killed it — but of course I did. And we both knew all the time that I would — and so would you. And therefore, even though it was only a conditioned reflex, and not premeditated murder — please, no weeping now. (2) This brings up two questions, which we will call — for the sake of simplicity — (a) and (b). Now, since I'm the one who first thought of the existence of these two questions, I hope, without hissing, that you'll excuse me for omitting consideration of (a). In any case, this is question (b): How come I just killed this roach with my wrist? In other words, *what's so special about wrist skin?* To answer this all-important question (b), I go around the room I'm in feeling everybody's skin from head to foot, stopping casually now and then at breasts and bottoms. Believe me, I only do it so as to make proper comparison with Wrist Skin! That's how I made this crucial discovery: that the skin on the wrist is different because *it is thinner there than any place else.* (3) Therefore I conclude that in hitting roaches with the wrist, what I was expressing was the last remnant of an increasingly anesthetized set of publicly conditioned feelings. This remnant is the one suggesting that if you *must* kill something, you ought at least FEEL SOME-THING — it is related to the publicly acceptable idea that it is morally worse to kill an individual with an atomic bomb than it is to wipe out an entire population using scissors, machetes, scimitars, piano wire, and rusty old razor blades. (4) This remnant also echoes the publicly respectable view of suicide. According to this, the reason why people enjoy killing themselves so much using wrist skin is that, that way, they are likelier to "feel something." Oh yes, it took the moralist's view of suicide to tell us that what assassination of the self represents is in fact Reverence for Life! And therefore, that the highest of human hopes must lie in suicide. (5) But what's that I hear? To all this, your only response is that you're still wondering what the answer to question (a) was? And also, you're wondering what question (a), itself, was? Oh, I knew it; I knew it! (6) Actually, there is a saving grace here, isn't there? Actually, we were trying to fool each other all the time, weren't we? I know: you knew all the time I should have killed it; but the truth, in point of fact, is that I didn't. And I have no idea why I didn't. And I have no idea what an individual like you would have done.

THE VORTEX OF HUMAN EXPERIENCE

(1) I read the other day in my copy of the magazine *Popular Philosophy*, to which I am a subscriber, that men ought to absorb experience continuously, like funnels. So immediately I tried as hard as I could to become a funnel. But because I had recently dropped my subscription to *Popular Mechanix* in order to subscribe to *Popular Philosophy*, and couldn't keep up with the latest developments in home and industry, I had mechanical failure. Instead of becoming a funnel I became an eggbeater. And I found I had even less of an idea of how to change back from an eggbeater to a funnel than I had of how to change to a funnel from an individual! (2) So I went to enroll in a crash course for people with my difficulty at my old alma mater, the Institute for Advanced Molecular Arts and Sciences. And soon, for the second time that season, I was ready to become a funnel. But this time I became a pair of handball gloves. My teacher says I'm making real progress! (3) Then one day, total success: I finally turn myself into a funnel. After all these months of withdrawal from my fellow man, I decide to celebrate at an all-University party. But when I get to the room in which the party is being held I see it is a banquet; there is a long white tablecloth with a long table under it and two rows of students facing each other over it, all with heads like funnels, all thirsting to absorb each other.

(1) Their famous curious position: almost everybody knows it; but of course almost nobody believes it. What they insist on is that it is better to give than to receive; and, by implication, that the best blessings are the ones denied, and by extension, that to reject and to donate are identical. They dream all their lives of such abandoned richness! Naturally, this subjects their sense of personal worth to the most outrageous inflation. Therefore, it is useful to the unprejudiced observer to consider whether these gifts they imagine they have denied were actually intended for them in the first place; also, whether if — should they eventually receive them — it will simply be because there was no one else around to give them to at the time. And if the latter happens to be true, why couldn't they have been asked to take these gifts into at least temporary safekeeping until the advent of the rightful owner? Couldn't they have been trusted? (2) In any case, because of their famous curious position, it must be that Christmas on Earth is here. The Children and I spend all day singing in the streets, making generous gestures along Fifth Avenue, and looking for the poor there with magnifying glasses. Also, all of us are leaning forward slightly, as if expecting something. But what is It? All we know for sure is that it is "gifts"; and that they must be coming from someplace else than *this*. (3) Yet why, every year so far, on the night after Christmas, do I have this vision of God getting up in the middle of the night, going to the bathroom, and flinching at finding the remains of all this tinsel on his nose? (4) And as for our Eastertime: it is an Interruption to the Resurrection. Here comes our old friend the Easter Bunny now: he is covered in black synthetic polyester fur, carrying two submarine guns, and occasionally taking target practice by firing into the air from the hip.

AVISO WARNING AVISO WARNING AVISO

Mole is giving only two kinds of Christmas gifts this year: one is going to himself, and the other is going to somebody else. It's easy to tell them apart too because the packages there at the rear of his gift-giving closet are clearly labelled; obviously it is very important that the shadowy packages not become mixed up. One is labelled "Suicide" and the other is labelled "Homicide." Imagine being one of Mole's closest friends and opening up Mole's suicide by mistake and Mole keeping your very own homicide for himself? Yet this is what the anxious, precocious infant-angel risks when too long before the holiday season she breaks into the closet to tear open these curiously wrapped gift-packages with the cards on them and marked with the explicit warning in black ink: "Please do not open until Christmas on Earth."

ON BECOMING A CHILD AGAIN

(1) There are clothings that make children out of their wearers — these light blue flannel pajamas with the ambiguous paisley pattern that you wear tonight are secretly the pastel pajamas with the lambs or rabbits on them that nearly everybody had as a child. So a bathing suit is simply a revised pair of short pants in which one dresses up to pay a visit to that invalid relative who nevertheless gets stronger every year, Old Mother Water. (2) And yesterday, the gesture of being covered up with a blanket by a gentle friend in a place I happened to be staying for one night nearly brought me up as far as the edge of tears . . . Also, shortly thereafter, while taking my customary morning constitutional promenade in fantasy, a pink rubber ball came bouncing my way from the heart of a stickball game; and then a black one from a handball game. And I stayed and played with the children for an entire quarter of an hour. And this actually happened in reality! (3) And I remember that years ago, sometimes on Sundays, passing the Childrens' Zoo where adults are not admitted unless accompanied by someone under ten, I wished I were a midget. (4) All these vital and crucial details of personal experience regarding pajamas are supplemented generally by the actual function of the human baby. The great human secret is that the human baby has never been created for abstract reasons: not to allow the human race to continue; not out of feelings of potential parental love; not even because of the celebrated joys of a supposedly good, careless, free, and non-prophylactic Fuck — but rather because of the one secret and actual belief that apparently human beings really do hold: i.e., that with regard to becoming a child again, the best way to proceed is to figure, SINCE YOU CAN'T ACTUALLY BECOME ONE, HAVE ONE.

INVITATION TO PREVIOUSLY UNINVITED GUESTS

A boxful of rare cigars . . . have one . . . and it melts into the roomful of unknown guests like a sugar cube melting on the tongue . . . like honey in the mind of the diabetic . . . like your wallet in the hands of a prostitute, like chopped chicken liver in the heart of the professional caterer, like surviving leaves in midwinter sleet, like ant feces in a vat full of nitrate, like an inexpensive tieclip before the onslaughts of rust, like conversation into silence among boring company, like the conception of generosity after December 26th, like space beneath even the tiniest hand caressing even the tallest lover from head to foot or like time in the mind of the sophisticated lover discovering the joys of some novel perversion, like the idea of 18th century chamber music in the heads of oppressed, like truth in a Latin-American newspaper, like dialogue in the mouth of the megalomaniac, like meaning in the mind of the poet. Whoever you are, my best, unseen guest, in case this poem is the first poem of mine in which we have had a chance at last to meet: please have a cigar; and also, may I offer you a light?

LAUGHTER IN THE SLAUGHTERHOUSE

(1) I know, I started out thinking that life on earth was a playground but then everything began turning into dirty-work, not excluding childhood games in the sandbox. When I was just a little younger I could shovel shit into the wind, and think it pleasant if among friends; even now, all I remember from my summer vacation labors in the abattoir is laughter at the slaughterhouse. (2) But then I suffered a change in priorities. I graduated from college and got my first job, a hard job in "The System": reading new manuscripts of verse printed on paper made out of the mist that falls among mulberry leaves; staring hard into space; and playing the harp. It was even worse than at the slaughterhouse! (3) And yesterday was my 21st birthday, only somebody burdened me with 21 dancing-girls all looking like Jane Fonda in the film *Barbarella* (1968) to fuck with or photograph or both, ALL IN THEIR NAUGHTIEST AND NICEST SCANT-IES! All it made me realize was that I wasn't even having a very good time at my very own birthday party! (4) A "human interest" news broadcaster hap-pened to hear about these feelings of epic exhaustion of mine; and so I was interviewed on national television. "Son," he began the program by enquiring, "wouldn't you say that you and all your kind are a bit — er — slothful?" I was just about to give him a logical explanation for this, the way I'm doing here, but then suddenly I looked down at his biceps below his rolled-up workingman's sleeves and saw that the poor man still had scars on his arms from selling too many apples in Eden during the Depression. That was when I realized that this was likely to be a very exhausting interview! (5) So how much energy have I left now? I'd like to try and describe my difficulties in detail but all I can think about is the endless number of little lip shapes necessary to pronounce one single sentence. So, from the sheer weight of saliva on my tongue, I sink to the floor. (6) Come to think of it, there is one thing I'd like to try and say. It's what Paradise would be like. It's easy to tell from here that it's a place where the only objects we would have to handle are concepts; ideas are solid there, and ideals like time and space, justice and truth, sympathy, humanity, brotherhood and love are just as real as everybody else on earth goes around pretending they are already anyway.

COLOMBIA AND HER ELECTRONIC CORNUCOPIA

She stands there on a little elevated prominence like a promontory, a large jar under her arm. It is Colombia's Cornucopia. She seems to be about to pour out the plenty we expect: loaves, fishes, licenses, permits, and exclusive franchises from the government for use in all forty-eight states plus Hawaii and Alaska. Around her in a ring are us multitudes, holding out our begging bowls on high. And sure enough, when she reaches suddenly beneath her horn of plenty we can see a little red switch there. The figure of plenty must be about to "Eject," as certain veteran beggars among us like to say. Already there is a loud humming sound — and then all the begging bowls fly into the air like so many owls! Then the humming sound becomes even louder, and merges gradually into wailing as all our other possessions fly into the air beside the begging bowls, including guitars, films by Godard, our secret Dylan basement tapes; also, our food is removed and our clothing is stripped off our bodies. And we can see that what the lady is holding is in fact a portable vacuum cleaner of considerable power. How come we didn't see the power cord running up the back of her dress? Soon she has sucked in everything and everybody, so that the earth is almost empty. Some day she might even have the power to suck up the curvature of the earth again, as a favor to contemporary utopians who still need to believe that the earth is flat. As for us, her formerly fervent admirers: we reside here inside the horn; and every month, promptly on the first, Colombia comes around like a landlord and reaches into the horn toward us to collect the rent. Occasionally, when we don't pay quickly enough, she reaches into the wrong end of the horn with her all-encompassing magic wand, and hits us all over the head. Most disconcerting of all: the horn also functions as an enormous ear-trumpet enabling us to hear the eager generations of the future already on their way to pay her a visit.

A LESSON IN OPTICS

"Mole," I cry, "what are you doing, actually coming out into the open so far, sticking your neck so far out of your burrow on such a sunny day?" Impatiently, Mole puts his hand on his hip: "Well, I've got sunglasses like everybody else, haven't I?" he asks. "But where are they, Miss Mole?" I teasingly enquire. "They're in this little box over my shoulder, silly," ever undaunted Mole announces proudly. "But Miss Mole, in order to get protection from the sun from sunglasses you have to *wear* them," I say. "Oh," says Mole, obviously very disappointed, "now I *see;* but really, I'd rather be caught dead than wearing these unsightly human things. Besides, for Christ's sake, I'll look like a *pusher!*" And he disappears down the Mole-hole — where it is rumored that he has also been collecting a wardrobe that you wear by keeping it in mothballs in a locked steamer trunk in a sunken vessel at the bottom of the sea.

THE INTERVIEW WITH TIME

"Say, Mr. Mole, for an 'exclusive,' why don't you tell our readers the truth about yourself for a change: for example, how come you're so pissed off about everything on earth all the time." That's what I hear the reporter from Time is coming to ask me this afternoon when we have our spontaneous interview in depth on the difference between 'polarization' and 'molarization.' The doorbell rings and sure enough, this little girl hops in with her eyes going around like fizzling pinwheels and carrying a gold-plated clipboard. She apologizes for being on Time and asks me if I'd like to beat her nice round tuchkas with a strap in the meantime. I must say, the interview is going better than I imagined! And after that, and a few moments of silent evening prayer, with me kneeling on her for a hour or two and she laughing a lot, she says we ought to begin our capsule interview. The first thing she wants to know is how come she has heard that my poetry is so freaky only to her it seems perfectly logical, straightforward, and realistic. "Is it," she wants to know, "the social realism of the soul?" THE SOCIAL REALISM OF THE SOUL? This must be heaven! What a woman! This must be love at last! Later on, when she gets up, I think I'll forget all about this polar and molar matter, and talk with her about my new theory of solar poetry. I'll save the discussion on the difference between polarization and molarization for next time, and the older reporter, the one I hear is coming from Time — no, no; I don't mean *Time* magazine, I mean Time itself, which, instead of a studious little girl with a notebook and gold-plated clipboard, is I hear going to send as a reporter some old guy with a scythe.

ANOTHER INTERVIEWER

Another Interviewer: "Mole, what have you been trying to say with all this sub-terranean mumbling?" Mole: "What I've said is what I've been trying to say. And I'll know what I've been trying to say when I finish saying it. In any case, we are the secret we are trying to tell, without prior knowledge."

THE VISION OF BLISS

Somewhere there is a place where location doesn't exist. Obviously I've been looking for it everywhere. But it isn't every place where you can see as much nothing as you could ever desire! You can recognize it easily enough, though, when you really arrive, because it has the singular and distinctive shape of shape-lessness; even after an eon of staring around there, all you notice is a dim sense of absent density. To even the casual observer, this is a dead giveaway. Best of all, as soon as even the casual observer conceives in the first place of the place where location doesn't exist, he can go straight there. And since it is a place which can only be located by a person who can *feel things,* it is also a place where people actually do feel things. And what I want to feel now most of all is a "general sense of heavenly bliss." But all that lands in my mind at this moment is this picture: it is a vision of bliss, the billboard outside the "Hot-Shot Klub" on 49th Street and Eighth Avenue in New York City; it pictures a scantily clad dancer raising her hand with a champagne glass in it, and bubbles coming out of the glass. We are there inside one of the bubbles. It is a place where the artists meet the businessmen meet the economists meet the psychologists meet the philosophers meet the politicians; and there, all together, as equals and brothers and sisters, everybody sells out . . . No! — this image itself must be sold, it is not enough bliss; think of the beloved, of being inside that place. Still, when I think of making love I have to think first of the jerks of her body as her pelvis retreats from the advent of the onslaught of pleasure, there's a scientific name for it, the name for it is a number on the juke-box at the "Hot-Shot Klub"; but I forget it. What was happiness here anyway? After making love all day, to show how happy she is, the beloved finally howls out in ecstacy, bellowing like a felled ox; then she bursts out into shrieks of "relieved" laughter, laughter that hurts her chest and your ears; then the color drains from her cheeks; and then her eye — swollen from too much "mischievous sparkling" — becomes full of tears and begins searching for the comfort of something tragic, — a junkyard, — or anyplace with broken things, and rusted or resisted objects to rest upon.

IN THE HOSPITAL

So we see the landscape of being alive at last! At last, after a long time of travel-ing we've arrived here, in the middle of the night, where we can really feel completely abandoned! Here anything visible turns out to be rocks. All there are, are these definite impressions, all so clear-cut that the shapes of the language needed to describe them threaten to cut off little pieces of the tongue, the lips, the chin, nose, hands, feet, and other organs. The subjects for which there are ideas, and the ideas for which there are subjects, all suggest that even in case of the most extreme suffering or torture, nobody ought to look for sympathy. Even down at the Hospital, on one of the brand-new deathbeds they have there — the ones with the built-in television sets — you might have to hold your own hand. And as for daily life, the way things are now, it is clear that the only things people feel like hearing about less than your illnesses, are your inconveniences. To heal the pain one depends on having enough medicine; for a complete cure, one waits for time and nothing else. Earlier expectations, the ones you had as an innocent invalid individual, were probably impossible anyway; didn't they come from theorists whose beliefs were celebrated to the degree that they were either un-believable or could not be realized? Now, at last, you yourself are responsible for whatever reverie you have left. And all you dream of now is a hand on your forehead during light fevers, the fevers which have always been your firmest impressions, the kind of fever you had as a child and which sent your parents back and forth down the hall to your bedroom on tiptoe all night. But besides this hand, you dream of one other thing: when you are well and running, an arm to keep you from falling. Even the metal one, with silver fingernails, which took such good care of you when you were asleep at the dentist. But on waking, as I do now at the end of this, defend yourself from memory; O Memory, when you and I were alone, and cried out in real or imagined pain, don't remind me now, when I feel like this, of a mother who never believed in weaknesses either; of the midnight angers of The Father.

THE CONCH-SHELL DOCTOR

For years and years the only doctor I had was the one I found in a small paper bag at the seashore one summer. He was a large conch shell, the kind celebrated for not being the kind the Shell Oil Company uses as an emblem. Still, despite this, I felt so sick that when I saw it lying there on the beach I picked it up from the water and placed it on top of an overturned lifeboat, the kind that lifeguards leave scattered around the beach to use when they need it, because they prefer a little littering of ships to one big one, of dead bodies. After I placed the conch shell on the lifeboat, I whispered into it regarding my secret ailment. And the conch shell whispered back a prescription in return! So I went to the drugstore to get the prescription filled. That night I applied the conch shell's recommended secret ointment, carefully spreading it all over my head as directed; and was completely cured. It has been seven years since then and obviously I'm feeling fine. Not only that, but I have the mental security of knowing that I'm receiving exceptional medical care, despite the fact that my doctor is not affiliated with the American Medical Association, Blue Cross, Blue Shield, or H.I.P. But then just last week I had another attack of my secret ailment. Thinking that I would need more secret ointment for my ailment, I went straight over to the Medical Arts Building on 57th Street, and up to the 77th floor, where my conch shell now has an office — as you might well imagine, after all this time word of his exceptional medical efficacy had begun to get around! The receptionist was not only pretty but also well spoken. "The Doctor will be with you in five minutes," she said, checking my name off on a long list of appointments. When I finally entered the Doctor's office I found myself in a beautiful pine-panelled room. As usual, the Doctor was smiling. I whispered my problem into his ear; and once again I was soothed by a helpful and healthful echo. "My advice to you," it said, "is that you pour boiling hot Campbell's Chicken Noodle Soup over your best friend." As you might well imagine, it felt better already to be receiving sound advice again from the conch-shell doctor! The doctor smiled his goodbyes and I went straight home and called up my best friend to invite him up for a little noontime snack. It went off like clockwork, too; I poured the hot soup over his head, and he punched me, then left. But still, for some reason, I'm not feeling too much better about things. What could be a logical explanation, I wondered. Perhaps, instead of hearing an echo from the conch shell that I thought was a prescription, what I heard was only the sound of backfiring from a 57th Street Crosstown bus? Or perhaps what gave me the original advice in the first place was not the conch shell but the overturned lifeboats, which are shaped like conch shells, and also echo. Or perhaps the logical thing to do would be to seek an alternative medical opinion, going back to the seashore again and enquiring with any random cockleshell? An upsetting thought in all this is that perhaps the best friend I picked to pour the boiling hot chicken soup over wasn't in fact my very best friend at all, but an impostor! My other good friends disagree.

ON THE OTHER SIDE OF THE EARTH WALL
"Break on through" — Jim Morrison & The Doors

"By the way, Mr. Mole, what are you doing all the time on the other side of that earth wall over there? Surely you've been over there long enough to know by now." To this, I hear a mole reply: "Well, one thing you do or rather *don't* do I can tell you about right off: you don't exactly spend all day staring back longingly to where you've been on the earth: at most, you *accidentally* notice things still going on back on the other side. Mostly you can just barely glimpse the tops of peoples' heads — here a dowdy lady's hat shaped like a flowerpot, there one with the top of a top hat; here a graduation-style mortarboard, there a beanie with a propeller on it; here a Mickey Mouse Club hat with a pair of big ears, there a set of Eskimo's earmuffs; here a cap from an army uniform, there a dunce cap; and occasionally, on state occasions — that is to say, on occasions when you're in a state — somebody comes by wearing a king's crown, a queen's coronet, or other formal tiara. However, during other times, during periods when social reform is desirable, what you see is a British colonial pith helmet plus two dark brown arms twining upward around a shapely scalp to balance the beauty of a water jug. And occasionally, sometime in the future, you will see the top of a head that is taller than usual, 150 feet tall in fact; and a head with blue hair surmounted by green antennae . . . And then, if you are lucky, you will see the tops of some smaller and more earthly figures running by in fear as fast as they can. But to us pragmatists now residing here on the other side of the wall, that's not so interesting as what we can see in *back* of us here . . . believe me, I realize that you want me to be realistic about what goes on here, too; that's so you can write the article about the infinite for *Look* magazine. So now, since you mention it; now, after spending all this time facing away from the far side of this wall and reporting back to you on Earth's future, *now* I'll turn and tell you what I see on the far side of this side of the wall, in back of where I am . . . No, wait a moment, give me just this one more moment to stare at the tops of these present heads, to examine the future of the present a little longer before I have to see about the future of the future. For the moment, for some reason, I feel so nostalgic about the figures with blue hair; let me dwell here a little longer on the old-fashioned charm of Green Antennae . . ."

THE TRUE 'MISS UNIVERSE' BEAUTY PAGEANT

At last, honesty in public events! — the Miss Universe contest really *is* a Miss Universe contest! — it has just been won hands down by altogether another creature, one whose advent was altogether unexpected, one who came down from the clouds in a space ship. She is a somewhat hermaphroditic lady with three green antennae, bat wings, tree bark for skin, with 1,557 perfectly formed breasts all over her body from head to claws. Still, I have to be honest about this: liberal as we try to be in such matters, I have nevertheless been inexplicably haunted by the feeling that on the farthest star somewhere, someone is outraged to have been omitted from consideration, and is stamping in rage with all her 3,224 shapely legs and 75,321 dainty toes.

TRAVEL ITEMS

It's really time now for your departure for the Other Dimension. But how do you pack for your travels? In the other dimension the physical needs are relatively modest: it calls for a thimble fifty feet tall, a replica of Plato's face to fit on the head of a pin; a baby carriage shaped like a shoe and whose bottom keeps on falling out, dumping Baby onto the floor. You won't have to worry about eating in the other dimension; but you should be prepared to eat the air, drink up witty remarks, and suck rocks. And for those most frivolous, mad, romantic moments of truth and celebration: all you will need is a decorative tree covered completely with artificial fruits and flowers of faith, something tentative to dance around until the real ones grow.

I. THE ARRIVAL OF TENTATIVENESS

Tentativeness is out in the kitchen now during the chef strike cooking up stink-bombs on the sly as fast as it possibly can. So the half-accidental gesture you make with your hand before your face when a bird flies straight at it out of the night, can also be a meaningful thing. But then this tentativeness puts on weight day and night; this acceptance of the approximate is hardness, after all; it is fat about the heart, it is the barley soup of remorse boiled a decade, it is a dream of nothing but rocks, it is why you hesitate here to meet and follow me, here on this mountain of relative values where once you were willing to climb until we were out of breath. So it must be time to come down now, in the end we suspect that tentativeness is our weakness; it is why forgetfulness is still legal.

II. THE OLD AGE OF TENTATIVENESS

Um ... Er ... Ah ... Every act you execute is some new kind of solidity. Even the gesture you once made in front of your eyes ... Something about a bird ... revise this! And if a second bird flew out of the night straight at your face, would you be able to improve on this gesture? The trouble with tentativeness is that it only moves as fast as it has to in order to produce the future; and when it moves, it takes so long packing its belongings for the trip that the taxi departs, and it refuses to carry its fifty-three trunks itself, it insists on remaining inconspicuous. For tentativeness is hesitation incognito; and hesitation is the initial and most primitive form of outright omission. Tentativeness is precisely why, all over the world, forgetfulness is so famous.

JOE

One morning, during this my illness, a voice was heard crying out down the street: "Hey Joe, Joe; hold it, hold it!" That was three years ago. What were they, down there, in the street? Garbage Men, with their truck. What in the world is going on? Finally it occurs to me: obviously, Joe must still be holding it.

FALLING ASLEEP BY A SILENT STREAM

(1) Ah, falling asleep by a silent stream . . . But then, crashing through the underbrush, comes the person known to us all as The Rampant Pencilpoint. He is a thin, bearded, literary-looking young man wearing the glasses worn by Tom Courtenay playing the revolutionary in the film version of *Doctor Zhivago* (1965). And he is riding a roaring motorcycle. Then he races off in another direction; and we go along with him, chasing an eraser. (2) But still, in sleep, we dream that the stream pouring past our heads is nourishing and cool; that now we are riding aloft on a silver spoon, sailing over a distant, silent sea of alphabet soup . . .

MUFFLED MOLE

Mr. Mole, how come you have fallen silent? Let Mole explain his behavior at last, in full, to even his closest friends! As for my own explanations, it occurs to me that perhaps he is silent because I just asked him this question while he was still talking, knowing full well that a mole is always silent on this particular point. No, a Mole never discusses why he is silent. Moreover, there is only one other possible explanation of this particular point: that a tiny butterfly has just flown into his ear and he is listening to it.

EMBODIMENT OF EMBEDDEDNESS

What if you thought that the best way to cross a wall was to systematically destroy everything on the side where you are, and opposite to where you wanted to be? And what if, after a while, you felt you ought to be all the way through, since nothing at all was left anymore on your side; but what if when you lifted your head you found that you were not only still in transit, but embedded halfway, stuck in the wall? That red overhead would not be the color of a new sky, then, but rather the tint of brick; and you are not seeing a new world, but the thickness in which you are sunken, in cross-section. In effect, you are buried alive! You cry out in a characteristic manner: "So this is how a white corpuscle must feel when improperly lodged in an inappropriate artery!" Some doctors are going by then; to them you cry out that you are engaged in useful and productive medical research! But when they hear voices coming out of the wall, the doctors go off to the doctor's, to get their heads examined. And to the left and right, despite the fact that you are stuck head first, you hear the clanging of gates; the shuffling footsteps of people going in and out; or else, worse, the sound of the open gates simply swinging back and forth, opening, in the wind.

UNDERSTANDING
Or, A MUCH BETTER PLACE FOR THE SAME PRICE

At last, some ultimate philosophical questions! (1) Is there any greater human humiliation than dining in the worst corner snack bar on the Upper West Side — the Remeldia Luncheonette at Broadway and 69th Street, and understanding that it is awful as you go there, but knowing also that you *have* to go there, because you don't have the cash to dine elsewhere? (2) Or is it a greater human humiliation to eat at the most terrible corner snack bar on the Upper West Side without at all understanding how absolutely awful it is in the first place? (3) And is it better or worse to be indifferent to the whole thing; and not even to care about going around the corner to the Ace Luncheonette, which you recall from past days, and which you *know* is really a much better place for the same price.

OF FALLING DOWN LOW

My artistic career started out well: I used to paint pictures of pornographic scenes on the toenails of aging chorus girls to keep them in a state of excitement while dancing. But prettty soon I hit the skids: I began to work for some public agency on a mural hopefully expressing "Hope."

TRAVEL NOTES

(1) Take me away from all this, take me away from all this! Away from all what? I don't see a thing around here, anymore, myself. No? Please look around harder, then; I'd love to know where whatever it is that was, went. After all, there must be something around here to get away from. And when you find it, please, hurry up and take me away from it. Unless, of course, there is something that it would be even more attractive to completely abandon. (2) In view of this, it seems logical to say that since it is impossible to arrive everywhere at once, we may have to accept being satisfied with being located here and there, occasionally.

THE LITTLE SPARKS

Now, at this very moment, close your eyes tight until the Little Sparks come, see each one hollow as a bubble; go inside further, enter the empty space where there is room in one, watch the curving walls revolving around you, let your mind move like that until the space in which you dwell is truly Belly, comfortable and enduring; so it endures until you feel that somehow, truly, you have become your own Mother.

GENEROUS GIFTS

Eventually, the truly generous giver may have an extraordinary experience: just as he is holding out his *right* hand to pass something to someone he thought might be able to use it, he will feel a sensation in his *left* hand. This sensation is as of a balloon of pure air from a child's lungs, being inflated suddenly within one's fist from a balloon-neck, visible dangling down from just as far away as one's own wrist.

STAMP OUT THE FLAMES

Stamp out the flames . . . stare at the shiny sides of your shoes for assurance that there really is no light left. Before the flames filled the field, there were no offers of assistance, so you put the fire out yourself; and you have kept it out all this time. But why do you still feel your neck bending in imitation of the flames that no longer remain, the few curls of smoke?

CHOO-CHOO

At the end of his train of thought stood the caboose, meaning. This is because most immediate meaning is usually the caboose at the end of the train of Possible Thought. But still, far out in the countryside, among the sentimental farms, all the ears of corn were waving! Also, the wind blew across the seat of the traveler's pants!

IN RETROSPECT REGARDING PANTS

What is all this heavy breathing about? Exhaustion after work, coitus, and birth is the only exhaustion some people will ever know. Still, nothing that exists has come to be without running the risk of remorse. Remember to tell yourself, and try to believe, that it is not the new thing which is ridiculous; it is remorse which is ridiculous.

MOLE IN HEAVEN

All at once a radiance from the ground — What's going on down there, what's happened; has Mole finally been transfigured, perhaps inadvertently but humanely, by gas from a fat drainpipe? Is Mole now in heaven? In any case, the yard itself is becoming transparent; you can begin to see down through the ground, layer by layer. First of all there are the lost things — all the missing valuables — the coins, the keys, the forgotten toys and souvenirs, shining with the pure radiance of every Restoration; and still, silhouetted, because of the greater brightness below and beyond, I can see a mole lying on a silver dais in the earth-palace, shrouded in light and surrounded by the faithful attendant glowworms; a chorus of tree and vine roots are singing together in the night; and then, gradually, all the Good Things of the Ground appear . . . Still, since everything is slippery as glass from the light now, the eye goes deeper and deeper, you can see the lost mineral deposits covered by frost . . . But no, I blink my eye and see that the "radiance" is only from an old Mole, lying on his back, asleep in his dome again, with a flashlight in his mouth. He must have been playing with the flashlight and it must have accidentally become switched on, while aiming straight upward, through a tunnel. But looking closely, now at least we can see the exact nature of a mole! Revelation, revelation, what a radiant revelation! — now we can see that he is approximately the size, shape, and color of an old paper bag that has been discarded and that has become buried in the earth without becoming crushed.

MOLE GETAWAY I

Oh Mole, at last you're going through, you're really going through the wall, in hopes of inserting a new earthly person in the world. Unfortunately, there is one more obstacle to overcome before they let you slip through: you have one foot left behind in this poem. And when the local farmers come up to you in their heavy boots, aiming the shotguns of definition, you keep on shaking and shaking the unfortunate foot. Oh, everybody remembers stories of fleeing creatures becoming enmeshed in fences and leaving feet behind as they leave! But here I come as fast as I can go to lift the fence and let you through . . . Only, what are you doing now, turning around that way, freed, yet staring at me with a long, concerned look, as if to ask, how come after all this I'm still here beside the fence, standing around and staying?

MOLE GETAWAY II

Mole decides it would be simpler to leave in a fast car. Oh yes, put on your traveling suit, jump into a pile of earth, and step on the gas! — Yessir, that's The Mole Getaway. Mole's circular vehicle, the same shape as the earth, and composed of ground crowded with natural gas and oils, minerals, dead vegetables, fossils, wet skeletons and dry wells, roars off across the night, careening in its independent direction.

THE NIGHT OF THE FOOT

In exorcism of my foot ill, 9/70, and in memory
of lost explorers and an astronaut

It is very dark tonight inside the foot. This is logical enough: isn't it one of the deepest regions of the body? It is so shadowy here that traveling through like this we can see only the light-colored objects: — the good bones moving around slowly, like travelers at half-fare, dignified, with shabby baggage; bones, but bad ones, slipping off like maniacs escaping from a train; bones still intact, but dipped in the deepest bitterness of foot blood; little yearning and loving bones signalling to hidden magnetic partners opposite them in nearby feet, constantly sliding back and forth so close yet so far away; bones dislocated, misplaced in the heel, fallen down great heights from the leg, lying for a long time broken at the bottom of the body like a fallen mountain climber; loose bones rattling around the ankle the way coins for a non-existent false cause rattle around a collection can in a sophisticated downtown "cinema"; mysteriously roving gypsy bones, jingling palpably as they roam back and forth from one end of the foot to the other; bones that travel in fragments, like a quarreling family on the money-saving Family Plan, wandering disconsolately over the famous and picturesque natural arch bridge; and there are bones that keep on detaching themselves with suspicious casualness, wandering like sailors along 43rd Street between Eighth Avenue and Broadway in New York City; and also there are veins: veins waiting for the Jules Verne, the Captains Nemo and Ahab, the Edgar Allan Poe, the Amelia Earhart, the Richard Halliburton, the Arthur Gordon Pym, the Virgil Grissom of bones, just to rupture.

APOTHEOSIS OF MOLE

(1) Mole is off the earth altogether now, flying through space like a projectile . . . his ears are folded back against his head, so he takes up even less space that way. He left five minutes ago after what was for him a long, fast take-off run of one mile an hour through the Mole-hole! At first he was worried about how many things he kept bumping into in this run; he kicked over the furniture, broke a bookcase, and even tipped over the ornamental vase containing the finest specimens of his worm collection. But apparently he doesn't care much anymore; you can tell by his ears and the way the whiskers are streaming out in back of him that already he is streamlined for pure thought. "Hey," I shout up at him, to make sure that my interpretation of his ears is correct, "what's it like to be streamlined for pure thought?" Then I hold the microphone cord up as far as it can reach. "What's it like?" I can hear him say as he ascends, "What's it like? — It's like agreeing with everything on earth instead of being so afflicted all the time, that's what it's like; it's like knowing that although at this present moment you disagree with everyone about almost everything, conditions might exist in the foreseeable future in which you could agree with everyone about almost everything; and, moreover, like knowing that if that happened someday, you wouldn't mind, or be embarrassed to agree with the other members of the race to which you supposedly belong." By this time, my arm following Mole is stretched out nearly a hundred feet long, and I'm running out of microphone cord. But Mole goes on, and I attempt to keep up with him as he continues: "But for now, being streamlined like this requires care, means making distinctions, means never agreeing automatically with anybody about anything, no matter how noble the cause or lofty the sympathy. And that's because out of all this, there is one thing you continue to remember: that as long as you have been alive, you have been responsible for every happiness that ever came to you, down to the smallest joy; but the contribution of everyone else has been a double gift, consisting of both happiness and grief." (2) Personally, I can tell that Mole is right about the role of other people, too. As he enters the stratosphere, he slows down because of all the air pollution up there, and begins delivering one last final speech; only I can't hear him, all I can think about is how miserable I am to be so alone now and how angry the station-manager will be because I've run out of microphone cord; and also how, because of Mole's eloquent ascension, my arm just fell off.

SHHH . . . SAYS THE SHREW

One day Mole appears at the door to his burrow. Amazing — Mole in the sun! And he thinks he's well dressed for the occasion, too, with his pair of sunglasses around his neck, his houndstooth blazer, his checked cloth cap pulled down low over his eyes, and his brightly colored carpet bag full of goodies at his side. Still, it's strange to see him; we've never seen a mole quite as near as this, and in the sun for so long. Mole, what are you doing outside in the air? we ask him. "I've decided to travel on to seek my fortune," Mole explains with what passes among moles as a jaunty air. But Mole, I ask, how come you're not traveling on using your favorite means of transportation — I mean, crawling around on all fours? "Because," says Mole, "I'm going to London to see the Queen." But Mole, I ask, what will you do for money? I can spare a little for you but not much. "Oh, don't worry about that," he says, "I've decided to sell my lovely worm collection — the one I understand you're going to make world famous with your writing — go on television, run for President, and then become a millionaire playboy." Then I notice: over one shoulder Mole has a stick with a sack at the end, as in certain childrens' books, at least one of which Mole must have seen during his lifetime of burrowing, stealing, and stacking up books. And inside the sack you can tell that there is a lot of squirming going on! But how will you travel on so far, dear Mole? I ask; I mean, we're not in England, anyone can tell there is no royalty here; and besides, the way you move over the earth, it will take you a month to travel even a mile. Then Mole points down to a detail I hadn't noticed: his seven-league boots, over his back claws! Mole is right; he'll probably make it that way; and how could I have missed seeing them in the first place? So I'd better be more careful about my observations; or else ask him about anything I want to know directly, from now on. But Mole, I say, won't you miss us all even a little, your dear friends or at least close associates in tunnelling, us gophers? Think of how much time we've spent together on the pages of Palmer's *Fieldbook of Mammals!*" "Shh, gopher, shh," the living-partner with whom I often burrow says from in back of me — "Shh: this is the way Moles behave when they know they are about to end their days on the earth they knew so well, or rather under the earth they knew so well, and before their final burial, in the air." Oh, is that true, Mole, I cry out at once; won't you even tell your oldest and closest friend, the gopher who admired you most? . . . believe me, Mole, it was you I admired, and not your valuable worm collection that I wanted to make my own, as some people I know have begun to go around saying . . . But already Mole is out of earshot; he is almost out of eyesight too; I can barely see him standing there, striding off as fast as he can go, head down against the wind and light. My last vision of him is as he gives me a final, casual, but happy wave with the bright yellow gloves he has on over his front paws — gloves which are, of course, seven-league too.

THE STATUE OF WILLOW

Holy Moley! Only 2,000 years have passed and already everybody's talking about the new statue on the green in the public park! It's just outside the courthouse in the space where the jail has just been torn down. The statue of course is a statue of Mole; what happened whenever Mole left his Mole-hole at night was that he had an entire secret life as a public figure. And though his life seemed to be lonely, it turned out that all the time he was accompanied by a biographer who as lovingly as it was possible for him noted down every detail of Mole's tale, down to the smallest. The Statue of Willow pictures Mole's departure: it shows him in his traveling outfit — the one surely everybody knows about by now, the one with all the old outmoded army knapsacks, the traveling cap, the cane, and the sharp suit. The sculptor must have been unusually insightful, because although it shows Mole in the position of being about to make a farewell speech yet refusing to make it, one can virtually hear the words he would have said. Also, this impression is supported and solidified by the fact that the statue has been made entirely out of willow. It stands there, silhouetted against the sun, one foot poised to leave, as if about to complete its earthly pilgrimage; but when the wind touches it, the least breeze disperses and dissipates it so that it looks like a whole series of people besides Mole — this morning it reminded me of a combination of Rudolf Valentino, Martin Luther King, Marilyn Monroe, Ann Blyth in *Mr. Peabody and the Mermaid* (1948), Robert Bly, Pablo Picasso, a broken hockey puck, Mae West, John F. Kennedy, Lennon-McCartney, Ho Chi Minh, a streamlined racing car, and the Famous Fonda family portrait; and also you, beloved. The rustling of these leaves is like Mole's speech: believe me, the rustling of all these leaves makes this less like a true picture of Mole when you look at it, than when you listen to it.

FOR MARIANNE

Now, make this metaphorical totem: A bump, on a little hill. Is it really true? — Have I finally been the one to make a molehill out of a mountain? And is it really true that poetry can create a thing as it states it? At least, for sure, some day the range of metaphor may be more than before; so that beyond making comparisons of things of more or less the same class on the same page, metaphor may associate separate states, and spaces over longer periods of time. Of course: *that connections exist between existing and improvised, visible and invisible, imagined and solid, lofty and low, modest and vast, past and future, true and untrue, real and unreal, the individual and this world — not to mention life and death — is only what is claimed twice a day by everyday public decree. But so far, who believes it?* Some day we may really be able to integrate our diversity, packing it up permanently and for good, so as to carry off *The Secret of The Portable Future* in one simple single shape; possibly one just like some shapely tree; or a typewriter case, or a suitcase, or a staircase; or a pencil-box or a burial-mound; or an animal sunken profoundly in the ground or a submarine submerged in the earth; or a dirigible encased in amber or an insect crashed on a hill; or an Indian dress economically designed yet decorated with the most elaborate patterning; or a tall rectangular turban enclosing the most sophisticated oval tangle of hair; or a forehead containing thought or a forearm containing veins; or a lady's compact complete with some cosmos of cosmetics or a picture-window looking out on the infinite; or even the shape I remember so well first seeing some time ago on your left-hand bosom, half-way up the right-hand side of the slope: this little brown mole.*